DELHI Heritage TOP 10

Forts

DELHI Heritage TOP 10

Forts

VIKRAMJIT SINGH ROOPRAI

NIYOGI BOOKS

Published by
NIYOGI BOOKS
Block D, Building No. 77,
Okhla Industrial Area, Phase-I,
New Delhi-110 020, INDIA
Tel: 91-11-26816301, 26818960
Email: niyogibooks@gmail.com
Website: www.niyogibooksindia.com

Cover illustration by Gurdev Singh

Editor: Anwesha Panda
Design: Shashi Bhushan Prasad

ISBN: 978-81-19626-75-5
Publication: 2024

Printed at Niyogi Offset Pvt. Ltd., New Delhi, India

CONTENTS

INTRODUCTION

1920 Archival photo of the lost fort of Qadm Sharif in Paharganj
Source: ASI Photo Archives

The word 'fort' comes from the Latin word *fortis*, which means 'strong' or 'valiant'. 'Fort' is used to describe a fortified building or a group of buildings, like a small town or a village. In Hindi, we use words like *kot* and *garh*, while the Persian word *qila* has perhaps become the more popular and colloquial term among the lot. Forts are usually associated with the defence mechanism of a governing body to safeguard a site or people. Forts can house garrisons, a king's palace, or even an entire city. In many cases, there have been strong fortifications around tombs, religious sites, water structures, or even in one case an empty ground reserved for an emergency.

Given this wide range of inclusions, it becomes difficult to tell which constructions qualify to be called a proper fort and which do not. In a few archival maps, various *idgah*s (open ground for mass gatherings during Islamic festivals) and a few *sarai*s are also shown as forts. Barracks/posts like that of Patparganj have also been depicted as proper forts. Most of these do not exist beyond the names of the localities. Lal Kot and

Qila-i-Rai Pithora have been clubbed together as the latter was created as an extension to the former and there has been a long debate on their demarcation. At the same time, Nai ka Kot and Adilabad, which were built as related structures, have been kept under separate heads, as at present time they stand far from each other and have their independent history.

For this book, only the buildings that have been recognised as forts by the Archaeological Survey of India or the State Archaeological Department have been considered. Further, the list was sorted based on the present state of the structure, its accessibility, past and present context, cleanliness, historic value, size and the percentage of the outer wall intact. The top 10 forts from an assorted list have been included in this book. While the major forts like Red Fort, Purana Qila, Tughlaqabad, Adilabad, Nai ka Kot, Najafgarh, etc. have been covered, smaller fortifications like Kotla Isa Khan, Kotla Mubarakpur and the lost walls of Qila Qadm Sharif, Naraina Fort and Kalka Garhi unfortunately have not made to the cut. I hope for an opportunity in the future to unearth them.

Throughout this book, one will find repeated references to few books written during the Sultanate,

Mughal or the British times. As a reader, one must be aware of these masterpieces. The oldest reference is to *Tarikh-i-Firoz Shahi*, which as the name suggests, is a historical biography of Firoz Shah Tughlaq. However, it offers much more than that. There are two authors, who have written a book each with same title. Zia-ud-Din Barani, the first author was a child during the times of Alauddin Khalji. He lived for first few years of Firoz Shah Tughlaq's reign and documented the first six years of his time at the throne. Barani mentions that his father and uncle were employed by the Khalji emperor. Perhaps this gave him an edge over others in his chronicling. There are mixed views about his narrative as he was sometimes considered to be biased towards his employer. Shams-i-Siraj Afif is the other author, who was contemporary to Feroz Shah Tughlaq and wrote his account under the same title, 'Tarikh-i-Firoz Shahi'.

Sir Syed Ahmed Khan (1817–1898) is a well celebrated figure in the Indian subcontinent. His work, *Asar-us-Sanadid*, is the oldest comprehensive work on Delhi's monuments and history. However, while reading this work, one would quickly conclude that he may have documented local fables and folktales as history. Sir Syed was requested to translate his work to English from Urdu by his British friends. As soon as he started, he realised that his work is full of errors. Instead of translating, he decided to come up with the second edition of his book. In the preface, he admitted to the mistakes in the first edition. However, even in the second edition, several narratives remain sketchy. For example, he is the first person to claim that the first storey of Qutub Minar was built by Prithviraj Chauhan as his daughter would climb up the tower to worship the river Yamuna. However, he did a wonderful job translating the inscriptions on all of Delhi's monuments and giving us some clarity into the historicity of a structure.

Maulvi Zafar Hasan was working with the Archaeological Survey of India in the early 1900s, when he was assigned the task of documenting every single stone of archaeological value in the region. He prepared a comprehensive report, which serves as the most important reference for any researcher. His book *Monuments of Delhi: Lasting Splendour of the Great Mughals and Others* was published in 1916 and includes all major buildings from the Rajput, Sultanate and the Mughal eras. He, however, focuses more on the technical aspects of the constructions rather than the history. This book is used till date by litigants in court when there is a property dispute and a monument is in vicinity.

Bashir-ud-din Ahmed, in 1919 published *Waqiaat-i-Dar-ul Huqumat-i-Delhi*. This book brings in references from several other books written in past. It seems that Ahmed had spent quality time researching and comparing different narratives. His work is by far the most authentic amongst all. From Cunningham to Ferishta, Ahmed has perhaps read almost every important historian who had written about Delhi and produced a comparative analysis. His work is originally in Urdu and has not been translated to any other language till date.

Other than these, there are several accounts by the British referred to in this book. As you go along, you will find the narratives interesting.

Vikramjit Singh Rooprai

Archival image of pietra dura detail from the Orpheus panel in the Diwan-i-Aam
Courtesy: ASI Photo Archives

RED FORT

QILA-I-MUALLA

On the auspicious day of 24 Rabi' II of 1058 Hijri (18 May 1648 CE), emperor Shahjahan accepted the invitation of Makarmat Khan, the construction superintendent for his new city, and entered his dream palace. It was the 20th year of his reign, and he had been waiting anxiously for this day. One can only anticipate his excitement when he took the journey from Kabul to Delhi. As he entered from the gate facing the Yamuna, Prince Dara Shikoh scattered gold and silver coins over his father's head. The entire palace was decorated, and the courtyards were covered with beautiful carpets and hangings, further covered by precious red Kashmiri shawls.

Facing page: Steps leading to Badru Darwaza under Asad Burj

Gordon Sanderson notes that,

> '...this palace became the envy of the art galleries of China. The roofs, walls, and colonnades of Diwan-i-Aam, where the emperor held his first court, were covered with velvet and silk from China and Turkestan, while a canopy, specially prepared at the royal factory in Ahmedabad for this occasion and measuring 64 meters by 41 meters and costing a lakh of rupees back then, was raised by 3000 men.'

This beautiful palace would hereafter be celebrated as the seat of the Mughal Empire, till the British takeover.

Chapter 2 of the *Gazetteer of Delhi District* (1883–84) begins with the battle of 1803. It reads: 'On 11th September 1803, the Mahrattas were defeated in the battle on the Hindan by General Lake; and three days afterwards the English entered Delhi as the real masters of the Mughal Empire.' After this, Emperor Shah Alam was assigned land from Delhi (Shahjahanabad) to the village of Palam (present day area surrounding the Delhi Airport). The British also paid a monthly pension of Rs 60,000 to the Emperor, to meet his personal expenses. Amounts ranging

View of Red Fort's Lahore Gate with barbican at night

between Rs 1,000 and 30,000 were paid to few other people in the palace, including his wives, children and the chief minister. In return, the Emperor will not interfere in the conduct of business by the British, who would now run his country, under his name and seal, without the obligation of even informing him of the decisions, until it is a capital punishment. Hence the epitaph:

'Saltanat-e-Shah Alam, az Dilli, ta Palam'
('Shah Alam is the Emperor, from Delhi to Palam')

The Red Fort, or Lal Qila, as we know it today, is probably the most documented fort in Delhi. It is the one fort that has the largest percentage of old buildings surviving till date, and that too mostly in decent shape. Like others, this fort was also plundered and damaged many times. It somehow survived the invaders and came up as one of the iconic structures in Delhi. It was the site of India's first war of Independence, and eventually became the icon of independent India.

This fort was not always known as 'Red Fort'. There is a long ongoing debate on its name. While most of the records suggest it was 'Qila-i-Mualla' and 'Qila-i-Mubarik', some historians have put forward a theory that it was also sometimes called 'Urdu-i-Mualla'. Prof. Shamsur Rehman Farooqi in his keynote address during a conference in Allahabad in 2014 helps us find the answer. He explained, how various historians and books, including the first Urdu dictionary *Farhang-e-Asifiyya* and later *Nur-ul-Lughat* have contributed to the corruption of the word 'Urdu' and made people believe that 'Urdu' is the name of a language. He suggests that 'Urdu-i-Mu'alla' was the name given to the city of Shahjahanabad, which we now call Old Delhi. Prof. Farooqi quoted many books and works of famous writers to reach this conclusion. But in his speech, wherever he gave the literal translation to the phrase 'Urdu-i-Mu'alla', he wrote 'the camp of exalted' or 'royal camp' and the language there was 'Urdu-i-Mu'alla ki Zubaan', the language of the court. While giving these translations, Prof. Farooqi quotes the work of lexicographers as John Shakespeare (1834) and Joseph Thompson (1838). It is perhaps due to these works and translations that some historians started believing that the court or the royal camp is called 'Urdu-i-Mu'alla', while in official records, it remained as 'Qila-i-Mu'alla'. The locals, however, liked calling it 'Qila-i-Mubarak' ('the Blessed Fort'). Interestingly, Maulvi Zafar Hasan in his famous listing of Delhi's monuments also mentions it as 'Lal Haveli' ('Red Mansion').

This new city was called 'Shahjahanabad' ('City of Shahjahan') and the wall that protected it became popular as 'Sheher-Panah' ('abode of the city'). In his book, *Shahjahanabad: The Sovereign City in Mughal India 1639–1739*, Stephen P. Blake recorded a very interesting anecdote about this name: After the Emperor took the tour of the city, he summoned superintendent Makarmat Khan and complained

1919 Archival view of Lahore Gate, as the mounds outside were being removed.
Source: ASI Photo Archives

that the city did not resemble the markets of Baghdad and Isfahan, as demanded by him. Makarmat Khan, on hearing this, dared to say, that he would pay the entire cost of the construction of this city to the imperial treasury if the Emperor agrees to name this city after him. Blake did not quote the reply by the Emperor though. It would have been interesting to read about the reaction of the Emperor and the court on such a blasphemous request. Perhaps the Emperor and Khan shared a special bond, as he continued to live a luxurious life long after.

Emperor Shahjahan had a desire to move his capital from Agra. After paying several visits to Delhi, he chose the site between the old forts of Salimgarh and Kotla-i-Feroz Shah. The foundation was laid on 12 Dhilhijjah, 1048 AH (16 April 1639, Saturday), as inscribed on Khwabgah in Red Fort. Shahnawaz Khan in *Maathir-ul-Umrah* has mentioned this date as 9 Muharram, 1049 (12 May 1639, Thursday). Sir Sayyid Ahmed Khan also confirms this date. He claims to have examined the horoscope of Red Fort, where the date of foundation is mentioned as claimed by Shahnawaz Khan. The fort was completed in nine years, three months, and a few days.

Bashir-ud-din Ahmed in his work *Waqiaat-i-Dar-ul Huqumat-i-Delhi* mentions that the construction of Red Fort was first assigned to Azt Khan, who prepared the foundation for the fort. However, in just five months and two days, he was transferred to Sindh. The work was then passed on to Alla Wardi Khan, who also built many structures in what we now identify as Old Gurgaon. Alla Wardi Khan raised the fort walls to 35 feet in two years, one month and fourteen days, before he was appointed as the Subedar of Bengal. The work then passed on to Makarmat Khan, who spent a little less than six years, thus making the duration of the whole construction time nine years in total.

The fort-palace faces the city of Jahanabad (or Shahjahanabad) on one side, and the river Yamuna on the other. Visitors enter from the city side, via Lahori Gate and proceed through the Chhatta Chowk market, towards Naubat Khana and the palace complex. Red Fort is no longer the same, as once built by Shahjahan. Its buildings were plundered and destroyed from time to time and new structures were added. Arcaded streets, corridors and connecting buildings have been removed, without which the existing structures have lost much of their meaning and beauty. The biggest block to vanish from Red Fort is the harem, which consisted of a few palaces, garden, mosque, market, and courts. A building known as Silver Palace finds reference in few records but is nowhere to be found. The storerooms, kitchen, regalia chambers and royal stables have also disappeared. Besides, there were numerous houses of the princes, nobles and servants, which are all gone. What is now left, is described in the following paragraphs.

Red Fort is an irregular octagon, with a 2.7 kilometres long wall, which is 33.5 metres high towards the city

Panoramic view of outer wall of Red Fort, taken from Matia Mahal

and 18 metres high towards the river. The fort is separated from the city by a 9.14 metres deep and 22.86 metres wide moat, which once had various species of fish in it. It measures 900 metres from north to south and 550 metres from east to west. The fort wall is made of rubble masonry and equipped with all medieval-era military requirements. There are circular bastions at regular intervals and octagonal bastions on corners, all crowned with *chhatris*.

Red Fort has five principal gates, out of which only three are currently functional. But the entry for the public is only allowed through the Lahore Gate (facing the city of Lahore, now in Pakistan), which is situated in the western wall, facing Chandni Chowk. In modern times, a security check post has been set up to the north of this gate, from where people walk through a barricaded corridor to the barbican of Lahore Gate (also known as Lahori Darwaza).

During Shahjahan's reign, this barbican did not exist. People walking in Chandni Chowk could see up to the Diwan-i-Aam, where the Emperor would hold his public court. For two hours each day, when the court used to be in progress, no man could ride an animal or cart in Chandni Chowk. Those who were walking on the street were to ensure that they do not turn their back towards the emperor and keep their heads down. This was a major cause of trouble for a commoner. Some historians suggested that Aurangzeb wanted a solution for this trouble and hence created a wall outside Lahore Gate. However, this claim has its loopholes. If he wanted privacy, he would have constructed a wall only outside Lahore Gate. But, he had commissioned one at Delhi Gate and one at Badru Gate too. This shows that these rectangular structures outside Delhi Gate and Lahore Gate were built due to security reasons. Emperor Shahjahan was under house arrest in Agra when

Barbican of Aurangzeb inside Lahore Gate, with modern lifts (tower on left)

these constructions were ongoing. When he heard about the additions, he wrote a letter to his son with the following text:

'Aye farzand aarajmand, Tumne qile ko dulhan banaya aur iska ghoonghat nikala.'
('Oh Son, trapped by greed, you have made this fort a bride with veil!')

Since 1947, the barbican at Lahore Gate has been used by the prime minister of India to mark Independence Day by unfurling the Indian national flag. While there are stairs that lead to the flag post, a few decades ago, two electric lifts were also added, to be used by the prime minister to reach to the top.

Original Lahore Gate

1961 Archival view of Lahore Gate, with windows and balcony. *Source: ASI Photo Archives*

1926 Archival view of Lahore Gate, showing a chimney poppong out of the wall. *Source: ASI Photo Archives*

Beyond the barbican is the original Lahori Darwaza. It has a 41-feet high and 24-feet wide arch. The gate is a three-storeyed structure, with rooms which used to serve as officers' quarters for the Englishmen. Before the British Resident officer was moved in there, it used to be occupied by courtiers. When Mirza Jahangir, son of Emperor Akbar Shah II, fired at the British resident officer, the lowermost rooms were given to the guards, who remained there till Independence. Post-Independence, the Indian Army occupied these rooms, until they vacated the fort on 22 December 2003. Old British period photographs show windows and a chimney popping out of the room. These openings are now sealed with matching red sandstone slabs.

Mughals were not maintaining a full army of their own. Instead, kings from princely states used to send their soldiers on a rotation basis for the security of the fort, or whenever the Emperor would demand. These army units always pitched their tents outside the Lahore Gate, in the area now known as the 15 August Park. There used to be a huge water tank, known as Lal Diggi. Tents were pitched around this water tank and the water was used for the daily needs of soldiers. Lal Diggi finds mention in few records, until the early 1900s.

Delhi Gate is situated on the south-west corner, towards the public parking. It is known as Delhi Gate, as it opens towards the older cities of Delhi (Mehrauli, Siri and Dilli Sher Shahi). It was considered as the royal gate, as it was only used by the Emperor to visit the city, or Masjid-i-Jahanuma (Jama Masjid) opposite it. The most attractive feature of Delhi Gate is the presence of two huge black elephants inside the

Above: Elephant erected by the British at Delhi Gate

Right: Original Delhi Darwaza with iconic elephants

1902 Archival pic of the original Elephant with rider, then placed in the Queen's Garden.
Courtesy: ASI Photo Archives

barbicans. There are many theories behind these elephants. Some say they were originally built by Akbar elsewhere and had mahouts (riders) on them, representing Rajput Kings Jaimal and Patta. However, many others reject this claim, stating that a Mughal emperor had no business creating elephants on the gates of his fort. However, one must remember that the elephants still exist on the rear gate of Fatehpur Sikri, which opens towards Hiran Minar; therefore the construction of an elephant was not alien to the Mughal architects. Another theory suggests that Aurangzeb had these elephants removed and crushed to pieces. They were lost with time, until 1863, when someone found them in 125 pieces, buried under an old building in Red Fort. They were then reconstructed in Queen's Garden (now Mahatma Gandhi Park), behind Chandni Chowk Metro Station. In 1892, the statues were moved to another place in Chandni Chowk, and almost a decade later, they were placed outside the Delhi Town Hall. In 1903, Lord Curzon decided to relocate them to their original position at Delhi Gate, but by now, the pieces were badly damaged and could not afford another relocation. Hence, the original pieces were sent to the then museum in Delhi, and replicas were erected by R.W. Mackenzie on the orders of Curzon. While most eyewitnesses, like Bernier, mention these elephants at the Delhi Gate, Sir Syed Ahmed Khan wrote in *Asar-us-Sanadid* that the elephants were placed outside Naubat Khana. This created a debate among historians. One reason for Sir Syed's confusion could be that the gate of Naubat Khana was also called 'Hatiya Pol' or 'Hathi Pul', (literally, 'Elephant Gate'). There is a passing reference of statues being placed at the Naubat Khana, but historians like Bashir-ud-din Ahmed gave a hint. According to him, dignitaries used to dismount from their elephant and horses at this point. Only the Emperor could cross this gate mounted on his elephant. Hence the name Hatiya Pol.

Both Delhi and Lahori Darwaza originally had wooden drawbridges, which were replaced during

Moat and bridge leading to Lahore Gate

the reign of the Mughal Emperor Akbar Shah II (ruled 1806 to 1837). The slab on the bridge outside Lahori Gate mentions that Dilawar-ud-Daulah Robert Macpherson Bahadur, Diler-Jung, constructed the bridge for the Emperor in 1811. Robert Macpherson was the English commandant of the royal guards of Emperor Akbar II. The exact phrase on the slab reads:

Slab installed on the bridge to Lahore Gate

'San 1225 hijri hua-wal-ghani 1811 iswi Dar-ehad shaah jam jaah Muhammad Akbar Shah badshaah Ghazi Sahab-i-Qiraan Saani ba-ehtamaam Dilawar-ud-Daulah Robert Macpherson Bahadur Diler Jung Pul faiz manzil tameer yaaft'

The third functional gate is the one connecting Red Fort with the fort of Salimgarh. A detailed description of the gate and its bridge is provided in the chapter on Salimgarh in this book. However, it is important to note that the original Salimgarh Darwaza is a few feet away from the current gate. The original gate opened towards a bridge of boats that connected Red Fort and Salimgarh Fort, through the channel of River Yamuna flowing between them. The British sealed

Original Salimgarh Gate
(now sealed at other end)

Entrance to Badru Darwaza, with dome of Asad Burj visible in background

this gate and built a higher gate, with a permanent bridge to the Fort, which exists till date.

Asad Burj in the southeast corner has a majestic opening towards the Yamuna. Bashir-ud-Din Ahmed mentions this gate as Badru Darwaza. The main burj (tower) was used by British officers as a residence and the gate was sealed by the British after a few attacks from this vulnerable corner. The Asad Burj also has an interesting role to play in history. During the famous battle of Patparganj in 1803, when Harnath Chela of

Badru Darwaza (left) with steps leading to it (right)

Holkar Army fought with Lt Col. David Ochterlony, this tower was severely damaged. It was repaired by the Mughal Emperor to be in its present form.

Another opening towards the Yamuna is under the Mussaman Burj, known as 'Khizri Darwaza' (literally 'Water Gate'). This gate played an important role during the First War of Independence in 1857 when the British officers wanted to use it to negotiate with the mutineers, who were stationed on the riverbank.

There used to be one more gate/wicket under the Rang Mahal, which was opened only when an emperor would die inside the Fort. This gate was known as 'Emperor's Gate' and was used to take his dead body out for burial. Gordon Sanderson suggests that this gate was sealed by the later Mughals.

Red Fort originally contained many zones separated by arcaded walls and gates. Many of these gates also had local names. These zones were divided, based on the status and rank of people living inside the palace.

Vaulted Market (Chhatta Bazar)

Facing page: 1911 Archival pic of Mussaman Burj, Diwan-i-Khas and Hammam (L-R) from river side. *Courtesy: ASI Photo Archives*

Some of these had their own gardens, fountains, wells and recreational arenas. Most of these were residential areas, with houses of royalty, nobles and staff. After 1857, the British started clearing these walls and converted the Red Fort to one large ground, with just a handful of original structures left. New barracks were constructed on the cleared-up land.

Presently, visitors enter from the Lahori Gate barbican and proceed to the vaulted market, known as Chhatta Bazaar. It is a 70.1-metre-long and 8.22-metre-wide double-storeyed corridor with 32 rooms. The ground floor has functioning shops, and a huge open octagon in the centre, known as Chhatta Chowk. In Shahjahan's chronicles, this market is mentioned as Bazar-i-Musaqqaf (the covered market), while the central opening is mentioned as the Chhatta Manzil (vaulted arcade). It was only during the reign of Akbar Shah II that the name appears as Chhatta Chowk in the records. This mention was by Bishop Heber, who had visited the Mughal Emperor, and was given a proper state welcome. He mentions Quranic inscriptions and floral patterns on the walls, which were painted over when the British took control of this fort. Recently, the Archaeological Survey of India decided to restore the corridor to its original glory. Several layers of lime were removed carefully using needles, to reveal the original Mughal period floral art. On both sides, behind the market, was a very congested residential block that housed the nobles and employees of the Mughal court. Bernier mentions that this area is so congested, that streets are just 4 feet wide. Even Bishop Heber mentions these houses and an 'exceedingly dirty stable yard'. Post 1857, these mud houses, and huts were removed to station artillery.

Chhatta Bazar opens into a large courtyard, which was once a square block with walls all around. It had a tank in the middle, always filled with water. This tank was connected to a canal, running along the north-south road of Red Fort. There were 4 openings, one being the gate of Chhatta Bazar, one being Hatiya Pol, the gate of Naubat Khana (Drum House), and two, connecting the arcaded road (north-south road), going from Salimgarh Gate to Delhi Gate. This arcaded road was also cleared post 1857 and all arcades and gates were removed. Barracks were built along this road, which still exists. Some of the barracks have been converted into museums and offices, being used by ASI and CISF. The canal running next to this road has dried up, but the trench can still be seen. Since all these walls and

arches have been removed, this square courtyard now has a simple garden with a road running around it, leading to the Naubat Khana Gate.

Naubat Khana, or Naqqar Khana, or the Drum House is a special building, which is present in all royal mansions across India. It is the welcome gate, where musicians sit and play music, sometimes all day long. Whenever a dignitary would arrive at the mansion, musicians at the Naubat Khana would beat drums and play special tunes to welcome the guest. In the case of the Red Fort, drums were beaten five times a day and other musicians would take turns in between. On Sundays, drums would play all day long. Bernier records in his memoir that this

Facing page: 1870 Archival view of Naubat Khana's Hatiya Pol. *Source: ASI Photo Archives*

Centre: 1931 Archival view of Hatiya Pol of Naubat Khana. *Source: ASI Photo Archives*

Above right: Hatiya Pol of Naubat Khana, from Diwan-i-Aam's lawns

1914 Archival view of tree at Naubat Khana, under which Britishers were killed in 1857. *Source: ASI Photo Archives*

day-long sound irritates him a lot, but over a period, he became so fond of it that he repeatedly praised the tune of drums coming from Naubat Khana. This hall of 70 × 46 finds mention in numerous stories associated with Red Fort and was also put to multiple uses since its construction. Two Mughal emperors, Farrukhsiyar (1719) and Alamgir II (1759) were assassinated here, and it also became a precursor to the events of 1857. What started as the drum house, was later converted to the War Museum, housing weapons from the Mughal and British period. ASI has now cleared it and the artefacts have been moved to newly restored barracks, converted to museums.

It must be noted that during the Mughal era, the entire square block, combined with four gates, arcaded walls and a tank was known as Naubat Khana. The drums were however played in the Hatiya Pol, the main gate, opening towards the Diwan-i-Aam. Since all other walls and gates were removed, leaving only the Hatiya Pol, this gate became popular as Naubat Khana. After crossing Naubat Khana, visitors encounter the first majestic building, known as the Diwan-i-Aam, the audience hall for commoners. This standalone building, measuring 24.4 X 12.2 metres contains a few rooms and a large hall. The main hall

Above: View of Diwan-i-Aam from Naubat Khana

Right: Aisles of Diwan-i-Aam, where the courtiers would stand during proceedings

is divided into three long bays, each with nine rows, making twenty-seven blocks in total. The red sandstone beamed roof rests on a system of columns that support the arches. In its glory days, the pillars were covered with *kamkhwab* fabric and there were silk curtains all around. Floors were laid with expensive carpets and huge canopies were erected around the building to save petitioners from heat. The building has now been robbed of its original gilding and stucco. All we have from the past is a few documented evidence and pictures from the British period. Bashir-ud-din Ahmed also mentions several rooms connected to this building, which were allotted to noblemen, who would be needed in the public assembly with the emperor. Ahmed informs that these rooms were levelled after 1857 and there is no way to estimate the size, shape, or extent of these chambers. He also mentions the plundering of the precious and semi-precious stones from the Diwan-i-Aam, and the vandalism of beautiful artwork in the building. During the Delhi Durbar of 1922, a wooden

1921 Archival view of Diwan-i-Aam with temporary gallery in the lawns. *Source: ASI Photo Archives*

gallery was added outside the Diwan-i-Aam, and an archival picture remains to date, testifying the temporary addition. The Prince of Wales, Edward (later Duke of Windsor), visited India between 17 November 1921 and 7 March 1922. On 16 February 1922, the Prince held a Durbar and a grand garden party in the Red Fort, which was attended by several

Rajas (Princes) of the princely states. The British records note how the Begum of Bhopal became a highlight at one point, as she was the only female ruler in the gathering and carried herself with much grace. Speeches of the rulers of Patiala, Bikaner and Gwalior were appreciated because of their perfect language. Jam Sahib of Nawanagar, Shri Ranjitsinhji (often known as Ranji Singh), the famous cricketer after whom the Ranji trophy was named, is also mentioned in several records for his fabulous speech. This durbar was attended by more than 250 dignitaries from all over India. While the rulers from Indian princely states sat on chairs within the Diwan-i-Am, facing the garden, the Prince of Wales sat on his throne placed at the same level, in front of the Mughal throne. Other guests sat in the wooden gallery made outside the building.

In the centre of the eastern wall is the Nashiman-i-Zill-e-ilahi (literally 'window for the shadow of God'), the high-rise seat of the emperor. It is a white-marble structure with Bengal-style roof and is beautifully decorated with pictures of flowers, fruits, and birds. It is said that the work was done by Austin de Bordeaux, a Florentine jeweller, who took refuge in Mughal court after he was declared a fugitive in his

Diwan-i-Aam at night

Top left: Emperor's Seat: Nashiman-i-Zill-e-ilahi in Diwan-i-Aam

Top right: 1902 Archival view of Moti Masjid. *Source: ASI Photo Archives*

own country. He also added the image of Orpheus, the Greek musical hero, behind the emperor's throne. Its pillars were once gilded with gold. Entrance to this elevated throne is from a small door behind the throne, connected to a palatial room and a flight of stairs. There is a decorated white marble table, measuring 7 × 2.3 in front of this platform, which was used by the prime minister to receive petitions and tributes for the emperor. Bashir-ud-din Ahmed also mentions that whenever a petitioner had to make a petition, he would take permission to step on this table and kiss the foot of the emperor's throne, which is carved in marble, a few feet above this table. Bernier, in his eyewitness records, mentions that the floor of the main hall was once covered with golden carpets and there was a silver railing that separated nobles from the emperor's throne. Common people stood outside the hall, under a canopy.

After crossing Diwan-i-Aam, we reach a huge lawn, which was once a complex arrangement of buildings and gardens. Today, instead of going through those arcaded corridors, we can simply cross the lawn, or walk through the passage to reach a series of buildings, spared from demolition by the British. The northern side, accessible to the public, has a huge garden with

Zafar Mahal in the Tank in Hayat Baksh garden. White marble Hira Mahal visible on left (distant) and Sawan pavillion on right

Top: Sawan pavillion, next to Moti Masjid

1902 Archival view of Zafar Mahal, with filled tank.
Source: ASI Photo Archives

Sawan and Bhado pavilions. These pavilions were important buildings of the royal garden known as 'Hayat Baksh'. However, from 1857 till 1904, this area was reduced to a dumping ground. It was a complex of two connected gardens, known as Hayat Baksh and Mehtab Bagh. Recently, Mehtab Bagh was excavated and the water channels were discovered. Hayat Baksh, however, was restored in 1911, after almost a decade of hard work on the orders of Lord Curzon, but only 60 per cent of the original garden was brought back. What used to be the central tank of the garden is now the western end of the complex. Sawan and Bhaado are marble pavilions on the north and south end of the water channel flowing through the garden. Equipped with beautiful fountains and a huge red sandstone palace, known as Zafar Mahal, in the middle of the tank is what makes this entire block so special.

Zafar Mahal was built by Emperor Bahadur Shah Zafar in 1842 in the middle of this huge tank of the Shahjahani era. It contains a hall in the centre and small rooms on the sides. The roof of the central hall is now gone and the bridge that connected this palace with the garden has also vanished. After the British took over, they used this tank as a swimming pool for their soldiers for many years, until it fell into disrepair and was filled with earth. Water was lifted into the Sawan and Bhado pavilions and used to fall through slits in the wall, running through the channel in the middle. Earthen lamps were lit in tiny alcoves in the wall, hiding behind the waterfall. This would light up the water channel and musicians would sit in these pavilions to add to the ambience.

On the northwest corner of the Mehtab Bagh, is a *baoli* (stepwell), which is said to be at least three centuries older than the Red Fort. It was included in the design of the fort and probably renovated to be

Stepwell (*Baoli*) of Red Fort

put to better use. This is a rare L-shaped structure, with its water tank in the southeast corner, further connected to the well. This *baoli* also served as a prison for the officers of the Indian National Army. Lower levels were covered with girders and slabs to create a huge platform and rooms were converted into a jail. After the independence of India, these officers were released from Salimgarh Fort, where they were shifted for trial. Indian Army continued to occupy the Red Fort and this *baoli* became the dumping site. When they moved out, the cleaning of this *baoli* started and it was restored to its original glory. This *baoli* is covered in detail, in a previous book from this series, titled *Delhi Heritage Top 10 Baolis*.

Moving eastward from the Mehtab Bagh and Hayat Baksh garden, we have a high-rise platform connecting the Shah Burj and the hammam. A water channel known as Nehr-i-Bahisht ('Canal of Heaven') flows through it, which also passes through various royal buildings on this level. Shah Burj on the northmost corner is not the same as it was originally. It faced severe damages during skirmishes of 1857 and was then almost destroyed during the earthquake of 1904. The tower was restored to its recent form post-1904. We have an incident from 1784, recorded by Bashir-ud-Din Ahmed, that Prince Jawan Bakht, after getting irritated with his father's strictness towards him, hung a series of turbans from this tower and ran away to Lucknow, to take refuge in the British camp.

Between the hammam and Shah Burj, on the platform, is a small pavilion known as Hira Mahal. This is one of the last buildings added by the Mughals. Bahadur Shah Zafar, the last emperor added Zafar Mahal, a well, and this Hira Mahal to the Hayat Baksh Garden.

Towards the south of Hira Mahal is the hammam. People often confuse hammam with the bathing place, whereas a hammam is much more than a mere Gusalkhana ('Bathing Place'). The hammam of Red Fort has three chambers, each further divided into two parts. The first one is known as 'Aqb Hammam' or 'Jam-i-Kun'. This is the place where the emperor would come and get undressed for the bath. It used to have three fountains, as mentioned in old records, however, only two can be seen in the present time. These fountains had sandal and rose-scented water flowing through them.

The second chamber is known as 'Darja Doom' or 'Sard Khana'. It has a tub for cold water bath and a

Darja Doom, with cold water tub and massage table

Top: Jam-i-Kun with one of the fountains

Facing page: Hira Mahal, on a platform, overlooking Yamuna

table for oil massage. The third chamber is 'Garam Khana', or the hot water chamber. This is from where the process of hammam would start. The first block in this chamber has small aqueducts under the white marble floor. Boiling water mixed with certain herbs would run through these water channels and steam would come out of the pores between the marble slabs. During the steam treatment, the first level of bathing was complete, where washing of the body was also done. The second block in this hot chamber is a tub, where the emperor would go and sit post the sauna. After the hot water bath, the emperor would move to the second chamber for oil massage and

1902 Archival photo of Moti Masjid.
Source: ASI Photo Archives

Facing page: Garam Khana of the hammam, with steam slab and hot water tub

Prayer wall of Moti Masjid with Mimbar (steps)

cold-water bath. After the bathing process is over, the emperor would return to the first chamber (Jam-i-Kun) to get dressed. Snacks and drinks were served to him as he sat next to the fountain, overlooking the Yamuna through the beautiful glass windows. The hammam walls were once inlaid with semi-precious stones and floral patterns.

To the west of the hammam is the Moti Masjid, a small 35-feet-long mosque built by Aurangzeb in 1659, for his personal use. Interestingly, Red Fort is not aligned with the direction of Mecca and hence a mosque would have been out of proportion concerning other structures. So, the architects created a box-like structure around the mosque, to maintain the aesthetics of the area. During the attack of 1857, the domes were damaged badly by a cannonball and were later repaired. However, they could not bring back the original golden cover and had to make a white-marble dome. The mosque has three bays and a small ablution zone in front of them. It appears to be a plain white lime plastered box from the outside, but from the inside, it is a beautiful white marble building, with exquisite carving and inlay work.

To the south of the hammam is a long-running platform with a series of buildings situated on it. These are all royal chambers, which were not demolished after 1857. The first building in the series is the Diwan-i-Khas, or the imperial courtroom, where the emperor would meet his nobles and take strategic decisions about the empire. This room has been ranked as the most beautiful room in India by almost everyone who visited it during its glory days. Ferguson writes, 'Even if this building is not the best in the world, there is no doubt that this hall is one of the most beautiful buildings erected by Shahjahan'. It is to be noted that this statement of Ferguson comes when he is aware of the Taj Mahal. This is the same hall, where the

(L-R) Diwan-i-Khas, Khwabgah & Tasbih Khana, Rang Mahal

emperor would sit on his famous peacock throne. A throne, that is said to have cost twice the construction cost of the entire Taj Mahal. Abdul Hamid Lahori, in his book *Badshahnama*, gives a detail of the jewels selected for Takht-e-Tawoos or more conveniently called, Peacock Throne and the gold used. The total comes out to be more than Rs 300 lakh. With precious stones like Koh-i-Noor (186 carats) and Taimur Ruby (283 carats) mounted on them, this throne became the most desirable possession anyone could have. When Nadir Shah sacked Delhi, he took away this throne and his successors distributed its gold, silver,

Diwan-i-Khas

diamonds, rubies and other precious stones amongst them. The Diwan-i-Khas is a large hall, with a virtual corridor around it. The ceiling is made of wood, with precious metal plates fixed on it in floral patterns. A few feet above the wooden ceiling is the actual roof, built of rubble masonry. The beauty of this building is well described by a Persian phrase inscribed on one of its inner arches:

'Agar Firdaus bar rooh-e-zamee'N ast,
hamee'N ast-o hamee'N ast-o hamee'N ast'
('If there is a paradise on earth, it is here, it is here, it is here.')

Further south from the Diwan-i-Khas is a set of multiple rooms, containing the Khwabgah (Bed Chamber), Tasbih Khana (Prayer Room), Toshakhana (Royal Wardrobe) and the famous Musamman Burj. This block is identified with its finely carved marble slab, fixed above the flowing water channel. The slab is so finely cut, that even light can penetrate through it. Symbol of the scale of justice is carved on this slab, along with a few floral patterns, to remind the emperor of always dispensing justice. These rooms

Left: Fine-cut marble slab at Khwabgah

Facing page: 1931 Archival view of Mussaman Burj and water gate, taken from river side. *Source: ASI Photo Archives*

were decorated with beautiful precious stones, which were vandalised and stolen over time. During restorations in past, colourful stone pieces were put to fill the cavities of inlay work, as recorded by Bashir-ud-Din in 1919. The Musamman Burj, or Burj-i-Tilla, or Khas Mahal is an octagonal tower, which gives Red Fort its iconic look from the back side. The dome of this tower was once covered with a copper sheet (*tilla*), which was further layered with gold. All of this was destroyed in 1857, and a new dome was constructed, which is painted white. The interior of this window, which overlooked the Yamuna, and the room behind that is adorned with several verses in Persian and floral patterns, most of which were originally painted with gold. The window in this dome that opens towards a ground between the fort and the river is similar to the jharokhas in the forts of Lahore and Agra, where the emperor would come daily to greet his subjects, who would wait outside the walls of the fort for hours, to have a glimpse of the king. There is a gate under this tower, which opens towards the Yamuna, known as the water gate (Khizri Darwaza). There have been attempts in past to open this gate and allow tourists to enter from this side. However, due to logistic issues, the proposal was never taken forward.

Further south on this level is the largest remaining public building of Red Fort—the Rang Mahal, or the hall of celebrations. Measuring 153 feet 6 inches × 69 feet 3 inches, this hall was designed to host various entertainment events for the emperor and his nobles. Its beauty was doubled with beautiful work on walls, a water channel flowing through the middle and several other fountains. It also had a mini garden within, as recorded by some historians. One can assume that the garden would have been more

Rang Mahal

like planters, placed along the pillars. The fountain in the middle of this hall appears like a blooming flower when viewed from the top. On windows and side arches, Mughals used to put curtains of *khus*, which were kept wet during summer. With flowing water channels, multiple fountains and wind penetrating through wet grass, this hall was often relatively pleasant, even in the scorching heat of Delhi.

Further south, beyond the platform, is the Mumtaz Mahal, which served as a museum for a long period. Records suggest that this building was briefly converted into prison immediately after 1857. A

1914 Archival view of Delhi Museum inside Mumtaz Mahal.
Source: ASI Photo Archives

painting in the museum shows the original glory of this building. Beautiful artworks inside the building were covered with lime plaster during the restoration of 1911. Recently, the Archaeological Survey of India has cleared this building, with a plan to relocate the museum to a barrack within the Red Fort. Wooden structures, like windows and doors, which were added later for the museum, have been removed.

When after 1857, the British took over the fort completely, they removed most of the buildings and made it more suitable for their use. Other than the

Renovated Mumtaz Mahal

Top: Mumtaz Mahal, before recent restoration

village inside the fort, the biggest block that vanished was the harem, where the ladies of the palace, including the emperor's wives, daughters, sisters, concubines, servants and slaves would live. This place had its own set of palaces, market, mosque, hammam, gardens, and entertainment zones. Other than the destruction of the harem, many windows and tunnels were permanently sealed. Barracks that were erected on newly vacated land were used by the Indian Army after Independence. When the army vacated the fort, ASI took over and established various offices, museums, and an institute in those barracks. The residence of the British governor-general became the residence of ASI's director general and the English church inside the Fort became the residence of superintending archaeologist of Delhi circle. These buildings were also vacated almost a decade back and now stand as empty halls.

From time to time, cleaning and restoration activities reveal new secrets of the fort. As you are reading this book, you can be sure that something new is being discovered on the other end of Old Delhi.

Red Fort Plan

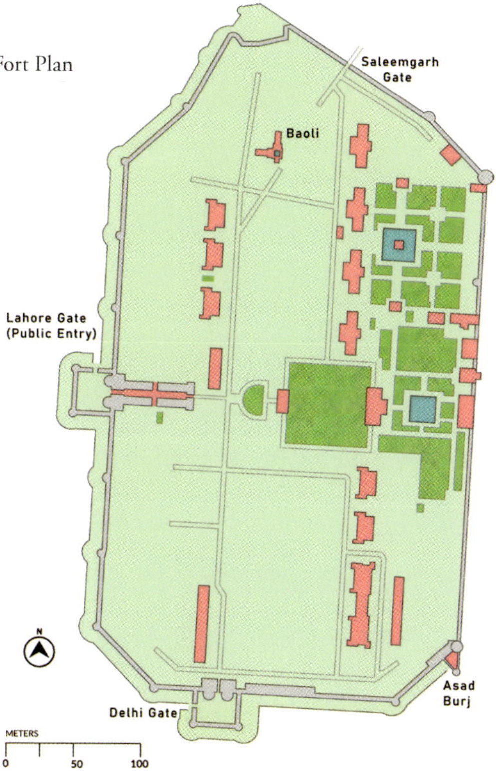

Location	Old Delhi (Shahjahanabad)
Period	Mughal
Public Access	Ticketed
Managing Authority	Archaeological Survey of India
Built by	Shahjahan
Latitude-Longitude	28.656246712385407, 77.23843793752036

PURANA QILA

SHERGARH

Purana Qila is allegedly the second most visited fort in Delhi. In most British era travel records, this fort has been mentioned in much detail. Many leading history and field guide books [*The Handbook of Delhi by Frederick Cooper* (Lahore, 1865); *The Delhi Almanac and Souvenir for the Year 1850* by Kunniah Lal (Delhi, 1850) [sic]; *A Handbook for Visitors to Delhi and Its Neighbourhood? by H. G. Keene* (Calcutta, 1882); *The New Guide to Delhi* by Lt. A. Harcourt (Allahabad, 1866)] mention Purana Qila as a 'must-visit' site. What is more interesting is that almost all records mention that the Purana Qila is said to have been built on the site of Indraprastha. According to the popular belief, it is one of the five villages that Lord Krishna asked from Duryodhana for the Pandavas. The villages that Krishna demanded were Paniprastha (present-day Panipat), Sonaprastha/Swarnprastha

Facing page: Talaqi Darwaza

(now Sonipat), Vrikshprastha (now Bagpat), Khandavprastha (now Delhi) and Tilaprastha (now Tilpat, Faridabad). The forest of Khandava was cleared to establish the new capital of the Pandavas, known as Indraprastha. What is even more interesting is the fact that in the BORI critical edition and the popular Nilkanth edition of the Mahabharat, these names do not appear. Instead, as per these versions, Krishna names four villages and leaves the fifth one to Duryodhana's choice. These four were Kusashtala, Vrikasthala, Makandi, and Varanavata. The Southern Recension contains Avisthala instead of Kusathala, and the word 'Makandi' is probably a corruption of 'Asandi'. No famous version of the Mahabharata in circulation contains the names mentioned earlier, thus linking it to Delhi.

As far as the name of Indraprastha is concerned, the most common belief is also rooted in a folktale. It is said that the forest of Khandava was inhabited by a tribe of Nagas. Their principal deity and protector is Lord Indra, the King of Gods. The Pandavas had to burn the entire forest and uproot this tribe, due to which they also had to fight and defeat Lord Indra with the help of Lord Krishna. When they built their city, they named it Indraprastha, saying that it is as

Archival view of Old Fort's Bada Darwaza.
Source: ASI Photo Archives

beautiful as heaven, the abode of Indra. Cunningham says that the word 'prastha' in the name refers to the 'prastha' of seed, which means a measuring unit of 48 double handfuls, or about two-thirds of a bushel (approximately 35–36 litres). Sir Syed Ahmed Khan, in his book *Asar-us-Sanadid*, mentions that the settler named it Indraprastha as he believed that this place was owned by Indra, the king of the sky. But Sir Syed also adds that Lord Indra distributed pearls with both his hands at some point in history and hence the name. While Sir Syed's work is important because it is the first-ever exhaustive compilation of Delhi's monuments, the only challenge it faces is that it relies on local folklore and hearsay only. Unfortunately, many later historians rely on Sir Syed's work, hence the stories mentioned in his book got copied into almost every piece of history written later without verification.

Sources before that of Sir Syed may not be a collective study of Delhi but do give critical information about the respective area they are addressing. For example, the claim of this area being Indraprastha is further strengthened by the map of the Greco-Roman mathematician and geographer Claudius Ptolemy, who in the 2nd century mentioned Indraprastha being a small town near Daidala, which was locally known as Dhillika. The word 'Dehli' or 'Delhi' appears to have arrived from this name. The area originally known as Dhillika is now known by the name 'Mehrauli'. While the claims of Purana Qila being on the site of Indraprastha are very strong, the archaeological evidence has revealed and re-dated it to the Northern Black Polish Ware (NBPW) era (~700 BCE). During the most recent excavation, we also found a domestic, palm-sized Vishnu statue, from the post-Gupta period (500 CE). There were small stray pieces of Painted Grey Ware culture (PGW) and archaeologists believe that if excavated further, we can reach the layer, which will put Delhi's date between the 6th and 12th century BCE. Alexander Cunningham estimated the date of original inhabitancy as mid-15th century BCE.

The fort that we now refer to as Purana Qila (or Old Fort) was the principal citadel of the sixth city of Delhi—Dilli Sher Shahi. After the death of Babur in 1530, the 22-year-old prince Nasir-ud-Din Muhammad was coronated as Emperor Humayun in Agra. He laid the foundation of a city called Dinpanah. Abul Fazl, in his book *Ain-i-Akbari*, mentions that 'Humayun restored the citadel of Indarpat and renamed it as Dinpanah'. Dwellings came around this citadel and formed a new city. Humayun ruled for 10 years before Sher Shah Suri took over. Suri further strengthened this fort and added new buildings to it. The residential area outside the citadel was fortified and this became the city of Delhi Sher Shahi.

Tarikh-i-Dawudi mentions that 'Sher Shah went to Delhi in 947 Hijri [1540 CE] and actuated by unworthy feelings he destroyed the fort of Alauddin, which stood in Siri, conspicuous for its strength and loftiness, and built on the banks of the Jun [Yamuna], between Firozabad [Feroz Shah Kotla] and Kilokhri, in the village of Indrapat'. J.D. Beglar in his report for Archaeological Survey of India (1871-72) writes, 'I am inclined to think that Muhammadans, as usual with them, availed themselves of the original Hindu Foundations in re-erecting the fort'. However, he also mentions that one needs to excavate the site to find out, whether he is right or not. This exhibits that the British historians were confident that all Muhammadan rulers destroyed Hindu structures. They perhaps ignored the fact that by the time Suri came to power, Delhi was loaded with Muslim structures and like many other kings, he would have dismantled previous cities (Muslim in this case), to build his new citadel. Also, he built a fort on the high mound, which gave him military advantage during battles. It was only recently when the site was excavated that archaeologists found evidence of a pre-existing city under that mound which had been buried for centuries.

Purana Qila's wall is oblong and an irregular rectangle in shape, with its eastern side being the longest. When it was built, the Yamuna used to flow closer

Lake, with the Wall of Old Fort

to this wall, but it has shifted its course by roughly 1 kilometre since then. Lengths of the northern, eastern, southern and western walls are 725, 2230, 1164 and 2040 feet respectively. Their heights are 51, 20, 48 and 55 feet on the inside and 71, 44, 54 and 72 feet on the outside respectively. There are three principal gates, one in each north, west and south walls. They are called Talaqi Darwaza, Bada Darwaza and Humayun Darwaza. There are four smaller doors/windows (wickets), three of them being on the eastern wall. Maulvi Zafar Hasan rightly mentions that it is very difficult to tell, how much of the wall is the work of Humayun and how much was done by Sher Shah Suri, for the architecture of these two periods is almost the same. Some historians believe is that the Walls and Gates were built by Emperor Humayun, while the inner structures are the work of Sher Shah Suri. This is challenged by the narratives of some other contemporary historians. *Tarikh-i-Sher Shah* tells us that Sher Shah died before the fort was completed. *Tarikh-i-Khan Jahani* adds to this, that Salim Shah Suri (aka Islam Shah Suri), who also built the fort of Salimgarh in Delhi, finished the Purana Qila. The walls of this fort are much stronger as compared to its predecessors.

Zafar Hasan comments that Talaqi Darwaza is one of the most striking structures of Delhi, with lofty *chhatri*s on the summit, standing majestically on the Delhi–Mathura Road. Right above the main arch is a window, which they may have used to shoot arrows or fire at the enemy. This window is enclosed in a frame of yellow and red sandstone. On its sides, are two oriels (projected balconies) in Rajasthani style. Above the oriels, we have images of lions fighting

Talaqi Darwaza from inside

with a man. These leogryphs are carved in white marble and between these two squares, is a long rectangular marble slab, probably meant for some inscription. Rooms on the first and second levels are decorated with plaster medallions. Traces on the exterior and interior show that this gate must have been decorated with glazed tiles when built. The door was repaired and opened in 1908 during the widening of the road.

Talaqi literally means 'separating'. And this gate has been kept locked for very long. Zafar Hasan records that there are numerous legends behind the closing of this gate. But he adds that there are no historical references to the same. This is where the archaeological evidence helps us. Zafar tells us that when in 1912, this gate was cleared of deposits and opened, several ink inscriptions were found in the recesses on the west side of the entrance, which were hidden for centuries under deposited mud. He says that most are just obliterated scribblings, but one is of particular interest, which bears the date 947 A.H. (1540–41 CE, first year of Sher Shah Suri's five-year rule). There is no scribbling after this date and the plaster hidden in there, where this inscription was found, was surprisingly clean. The only explanation is that the gate was never opened after it was closed sometime in 1541 or soon after. The plaster at such places is exactly as it was when they first built the gate. However, in all other areas, the plaster had developed major cracks and even a small portion of the bastion of the gate had collapsed. Zafar

Talaqi Darwaza from inside

also suggests that this gate, like other gates, was closed to protect the fort. One inscription found there translated to: 'O God! Preserve this house of Humayun from damage'. Since Suri was the ruling emperor at this time, it is unlikely that the person who scribbled that line was referring to Mughal emperor Humayun. He probably meant the literal translation of the word 'Humayun', which is 'auspicious'. Or was he hinting that the original builder is Humayun? When cleared, the archaeologists noticed that there was no weapon or artillery buried in there. This means, the gate never served its original purpose of protecting the fort.

The first floor of Talaqi Darwaza had large wooden doors for the rooms, which were two-leafed and studded with large nails. Owing to their bad condition, they were removed in 1912. The same year, during restoration, two proposals were submitted to the government. One was to construct a lake in front of the Fort, from Talaqi Darwaza to the main entrance, the Bada Darwaza, and the other was to divert a stream from the Yamuna and create a moat around the fort. As seen in present times, we know that the first proposal was accepted. The gate on the inner side appears like an amphitheatre with semi-circular steps. These steps were not there originally but were added sometime later. Zafar Hasan mentions these steps at Talaqi and Humayun Darwaza, which proves that they were added before the beginning of the 20th century. He also mentions that the passage between the two gates is not part of the original design of the fort.

On the southern wall, facing the National Zoological Park, is the Humayun Gate. Carr Stephen thinks that it is not worthy of notice. However, the elements on this gate are equally striking and have unique features. This gate was also blocked for long and got cleared much later only in 1914. On the outside, this gate matches Talaqi Darwaza in design, except that in place of the lion images, it contains realistically carved elephants. An inscription on the gate, as stated by Maulvi Zafar Hasan, mentions that this gate was built by Ghazi Khan Lohani in the year 950 AH (1543–44 CE), during the reign of Sher Shah Suri. While not much is known of Ghazi Khan, we are aware that the Lohanis were influential since the Lodhi era in the politics of Delhi and Agra.

One theory behind the name Humayun Darwaza is that the gate is called so since the body of Emperor Humayun was transported through this gate in 1556 to his final resting place. Light and Sound Show of Purana Qila is organised on the inner side of this gate every evening.

While Humayun and Talaqi Darwaza have been kept locked for long, Bada Darwaza has been functional. It is situated on the western wall and shares the entry road

Bada Darwaza, the present entry to Fort

with National Zoological Park. During restoration in the early 1900s, archaeologists discovered the traces of a wooden drawbridge, which was replaced with a permanent causeway in the 1890s. The Bada Darwaza is slightly different in design from the other two gates, and has two hexagrams as medallions on the corners of the main arch.

The mosque inside the fort is known as Qila-i-Kuhna Masjid (literally 'Mosque of the Ancient Fort'). Everyone who wrote about it describes it as one of

Qila-i-Kuhan Mosque with ablution tank in front

the finest masterpieces of the architecture of Sur Dynasty. When one looks at the structure in person, only then it becomes clear. *Tarikh-i-Dawudi* and *Tarikh-i-Sher Shahi* mention that a lot of gold, silver and lapis lazuli was used in its construction. The mosque can be seen from the road between Pragati Maidan and Old Fort, as you approach the Bhairon Temple. In olden days, when the Yamuna used to flow closer to the fort, the sight of a strong wall and a majestic mosque projecting out at one end must have made a great impression. It has a hall of size 168 feet by 48 feet 9 inches with five chambers. Ferguson calls its arches to be of Tudor form. Just outside the mosque, we have a 16-sided ablution tank. Zafar Hasan suggests that there may have been a fountain in the tank at some point in time. A balanced blend of black, white marble and red sandstone on walls make this mosque more attractive. Projected balconies (oriels) are a unique element of its design. The western wall is projected outwards from the central chamber and has buttresses on either side. Edges of the western wall are infused with three-storeyed half-octagon towers containing windows with beautifully carved corbelled arches. Interestingly, this is the only mosque from this period to have this type of design. The other mosque to have some of these elements is the Moth ki Masjid from the Lodhi period, situated in Uday Park, South Ex II.

Qila-i-Kuhna mosque has one large dome, but Maulvi Zafar Hasan mentions that there were two additional domes on either side. These smaller domes, though disappeared by Sir Syed's time, were referenced by him too. In the illustration provided in *Asar-us-Sanadid*, one can see two platforms, which would have housed the said domes. At present time, even these platforms don't exist. During the massive

1914 Archival view of the dome of Qila-i-Kuhna mosque.
Source: ASI Photo Archives

earthquake of 1905, the mosque was badly damaged and there is a possibility that during repair, some elements got modified. Dr Vogel gave a theory that the two outermost compartments in this mosque were built during a later period to expand it. He based his claim on the fact that the material, style and size of the last two compartments are different from the three main compartments. Staircases in the northern and southern walls take you to the upper level, which is connected to a corridor around the central dome, and further reaches the roof.

An inscription on the marble slab on the second arch towards north reads, 'As long as the world is populated, may this edifice be frequented, and may the people of the world be cheerful and happy in it.'

The marble slab on the second arch towards the south reads: 'Oh God! Show mercy for we are polluted, and our liver is washed with the blood of our heart. Instruct us as is best in thy sight for we have been wanting in our duties.'

Another important structure in Purana Qila is the two-storeyed octagonal tower known as Shermandal. With a diametre of 53 feet and each side measuring 21 feet 9 inches, this is a relatively small building, but the incident associated with it makes it far more noteworthy. Almost all historians from the time of Akbar state that on the 8th of Rabi-ul-Awwal, at sunset, Emperor Humayun went to the roof of the library, and while he was there, he heard the azan by the muezzin. He was coming down and had reached just the second step. The emperor immediately sat on the step for prayer and while he was getting up, his foot slipped and he fell, badly injuring his head. While most historians do not explicitly mention Sher Mandal, Akbarnamah mentions that this building of

Sher Mandal

Sher Mandal was utilised as the library for emperor Humayun. On 15th Rabiul Awwal 963 AH (24th January 1556), Emperor Humayun left this world. He was buried within the Old Fort until his tomb, to the south of this fort, was near completion and the body was moved to its final resting place in what we now know as the Humayun's Tomb. No historian or archaeologist provides an accurate account of the use of this building before Emperor Humayun took over. There are multiple theories, and they all agree to the fact that it was built by Sher Shah Suri. Some suggested that it was surrounded by other lofty palatial structures, which cannot be true as the design of the building is such, that it should remain on a high mound, isolated, to embrace the breeze and view. Besides, no remains of any connected structure were found around it during restoration or excavation. *Tarikh-i-Dawudi* however mentions that 'in the middle of a fort, there is a building of Sher Shah called the Sher Mandal, which is left incomplete.'

In 1892, there was a proposal to allocate land within the premise of Purana Qila for the burial ground of the Baptist Mission to India. References of Lahore and some other parts of Punjab were given, where similar cemeteries were built. However, it seems that this proposal was never accepted.

Old records suggest that the southern half of the fort was entirely occupied by a village, which was removed when the British moved their capital to Delhi. Villagers built houses and even occupied many of the arched rooms in the wall of the fort. In March 1913, all the houses were acquired by the British

Facing page above: 1923 Archival view of the temple before restoration. *Source: ASI Photo Archives*

Facing page below: 1926 Archival view of Temple after restoration. *Source: ASI Photo Archives*

government and their 1900 occupants were relocated to Rohtak, Bulandshahar and Gurgaon. Maulvi Zafar Hasan mentions that these families were given a compensation of Rs 1,44,183. All correspondence regarding this, which happened between Hailey, Sanderson and Beadon, is preserved at the Delhi Archives. It is mentioned that the people living there are tenants of the Municipal Committee and pay rent. However, some of them have stored tobacco in the bastions and locked them. These bastions and walls, though, require immediate repair. Since the villagers were not letting archaeologists in, they requested the deputy commissioner to have the villagers removed. As this congested village was cleared and modern houses were removed, several historic secrets were revealed. Most interesting amongst these was the garbage pit of the village. When it was cleared, it turned out to be a 73-feet deep stepwell. After the stepwell was restored, the water returned, and even today, it is used to irrigate the lawns of Purana Qila. Another structure that revealed itself from under a house was a Mughal-era hammam. A well opposite the principal mosque of the fort was also found.

Often, interesting structures are hidden in plain sight. The Kunti Devi Temple in Purana Qila is one such edifice. As we enter from the main gate of the fort and proceed to Sher Mandal, in the lawn to our right stands a large walled compound, said to have been the temple originally built by Kunti Devi, mother of Pandavas. The present structure, however, is from 1994 and was built by Pt. Ghyasi Ram Bhardwaj. Presiding deities are Lord Shiva and Durga. Maulvi Zafar Hasan states in his record that an old inscription found in this temple mentions one Lai Bahadur Singh [sic] to have purchased 12 bighas of land here (or in the vicinity) and built this temple in honour of Lord Krishna, during the reign of Emperor Akbar II (1806–1837).

At the beginning of the 1900s, when John Marshall, the then Director-General of Archaeological Survey of India, was conducting a cleaning process in the Old Fort, they discovered bricks measuring 12 × 12 inches and 3 inches thick. He estimated the date to be between the 4th and 7th century CE (Gupta Period). Later, a trial excavation was conducted by B.B. Lal in 1954–55, where he found painted grey ware traces in form of dishes and bowls. He also discovered houses with kiln-burnt bricks, terracotta ring wells, iron implements, copper-cast coins and punch-marked coins. This takes the period of settlement beyond 600

Excavation site in 2014

BCE. The excavation work was not completed then, hence the ASI resumed work in 1969, which continued till 1973. It was conducted under the direction of B.B. Lal, B.K. Thapar, M.C. Joshi and N.C. Ghosh. As they excavated the portion between the Sher Mandal and eastern wall, they found layers of almost every period in history since 1200 BCE. Details about these excavations can be found in ASI's respective reports and an overview can be read in Dr B.R. Mani's book *Delhi: Threshold of the Orient*, published in 1997. Dr Mani, while working with ASI, was instrumental in many excavations in Delhi. After Dr Mani retired from ASI, further excavations were conducted in the fort. The most recent one was headed by Sh. Vasant Swarnkar that concluded in 2017. His team was able to find coins, statues and further traces of civilisation in the region. This proves that Purana Qila stands on the site of an ancient town.

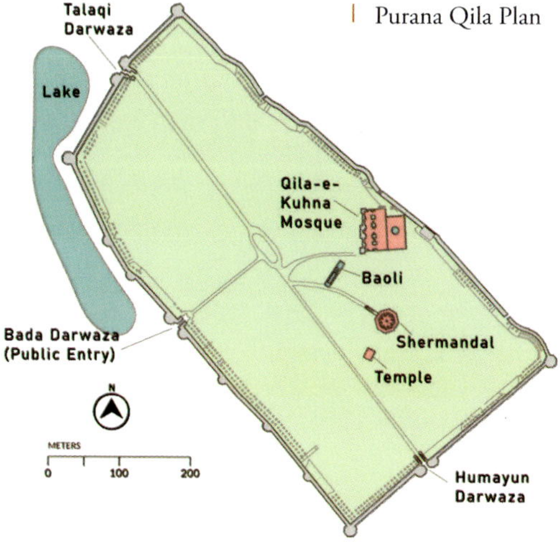

Purana Qila Plan

Location	Mathura Road, Near Pragati Maidan
Period	Afghan
Public Access	Ticketed
Managing Authority	Archaeological Survey of India
Built by	Humayun/Sher Shah Suri
Latitude-Longitude	28.60885448814699, 77.24222108078183

TUGHLAQABAD

Ruins of Tughlaqabad

'O great Sultan, master of the world, you are the most powerful and invincible. Why don't you commission a bigger and better fort on that nearby hill to celebrate your mightiness?' said Ghazi Malik to his master, the Sultan of Delhi. Khilji, his master, being an arrogant and self-centred king, mocked him, 'You can build one when you become the king.' And fate had its way. Khilji dynasty ended, and Ghazi Malik was coronated as Sultan Ghiasuddin Tughlaq, thus starting the Tughlaq Dynasty of Delhi Sultanate. Without wasting much time, the new Sultan commissioned his dream fort on the hill between Siri and Tilpat (later Faridabad).

This is the most common folktale narrated by the storytellers in association with the origin of the fort-city of Tughlaqabad. It is mentioned in the memoirs of Ibn Battuta, the famous Moroccan traveller, who visited Delhi during the reign of Muhammad Bin Tughlaq and was also appointed as the Qazi of Delhi. But this is not the only story connected to this fort. Tughlaqabad is the largest surviving one of all the forts in Delhi. Despite of its majestic size, the fort was built in just two years from the laying of the foundation in 1321. Tughlaq left no stone unturned to arrange for resources to finish this project. This caused a major rift between the Emperor and the Sufi mystic Khwaja Nizamuddin Auliya. The drift grew so much that, it is said, the saint cursed this fort to always remain abandoned or be inhabited by goat herders. A detailed account of this incident can be found in the chapter on Nizam-ud-Din Baoli in the book *Delhi Heritage Top 10 Baolis*.

The Sultan was no ordinary fighter during his early days. He was feared by many from Afghanistan to Telangana. It was he who established a strong protective shield to save Delhi from the continuous Mughal (Mongol) invasions during the Khilji regime. Zia-ud-din Barani, in his work *Tarikh-i-Firoz Shahi* mentions that Ghazi Malik, who later became Sultan Tughlaq Shah, was well known in Hindustan and Khorasan (part of Central Asia, Afghanistan and Iran). He took care of Dipalpur and Lahore (both in present-day Pakistan), which served as the entry point for Mughal (Mongol) invaders. Every winter, he would march out with his army to the Mughal frontiers in Khorasan and challenge them.

It eventually created such a fear of Ghazi Malik amongst the invaders that they did not even dare to maintain proper military posts on the frontiers. Until then, Delhi had seen countless attacks by these tribes. The invading armies were defeated every time, but at the cost of many lives and resources on both sides. It had become a pain for the Khilji to run the empire. But after Ghazi Malik strengthened the frontier of the empire, the fear was so high that even during the rule of Qutubuddin Mubarak Khilji, when the court was at its weakest point, no invader dared to enter Hindustan.

Tughlaqabad Wall, as seen from Tughlaq's Tomb

When the last emperor of the Khilji dynasty was assassinated, the rebel Khusro Khan ascended to the throne in Siri Fort. Ghazi Malik, upon hearing about the death of his master, waited for some time, as his son Jauna Khan (later Muhammad Bin Tughlaq) was inside the palace and Khusro Khan could hurt him. But when Jauna Khan escaped, Ghazi Malik

was able to charge at Delhi and take over. Khusro Khan was removed and nobles established Ghazi Malik as the new Sultan of Delhi. He ruled for four years only, from 1321 to 1325. During this period, he proved to be a king, whom everyone must fear. To finish his dream project, the fort of Tughlaqabad, he ordered that every available labourer should immediately report to Delhi and work for the emperor.

The outer fortification is an irregular rhombus, approximately 6 km long and covers almost 2 sq. km. of the area. This was the city of Tughlaqabad. Within this city, there is a strong fortified enclosure in the western corner. This enclosure used to be a fort for army and nobles. This portion is approximately 2.9 km long and covers about 0.3 sq. km of area. There is a third level of fortification, within this second layer. It falls towards the south end of this second layer of the fort. It is the highest point of this city and is also sometimes referred to as Bijai Mandal (or Burj Mandal). It has

Walls of Tughlaqabad, with causeway between Tomb & Fort visible

a strong wall with bastions and a strategically placed staircase. The wall is roughly 800 metres long and provides excellent protection for soldiers manning the watchtower. Even today, it is one of the most important points in the fort as it provides a panoramic view of Tughlaqabad and surrounding areas. Sir Syed Ahmed says that the city (of Tughlaqabad) had 52

gates, but only 13 were traced. Out of these, only 9 were identified. These are Delhi Gate, Nimwala Gate and Dhoban Gate to the west; Chaklakhana Gate to the north; Bhati Gate, Rawal Gate and Bindaoli Gate to the east; and Andheri Gate and Hatya (or Hathi) Gate to the south. Huge stones were arranged to create the wall of this fort. Bashir-ud-Din Ahmed records that the largest stone piece measured here was 14 feet long and 2.5 feet wide and it weighed 6 tonnes. Maulvi Zafar writes that the walls at many places are about 90 feet high. Some of the writers from the British period seemed amused at the mere thought of getting such big stones and creating huge walls on top of a hill, that too several centuries ago, without the so-called technological boom.

J.D. Beglar in his report for Archaeological Survey of India (1871–72) writes that city was full of houses that had rooms and a single-entry door. The door always opened into a courtyard measuring 22 feet by 12 feet. In some cases, this courtyard also had one or two

Above: 1923 Archival view of Andheri Gate of Tughlaqabad, from South East. *Source: ASI Photo Archives*

Above centre: 1920 Archival view of a Gate in South wall of Tughlaqabad. *Source: ASI Photo Archives*

Above right: Mosque inside Tughlaqabad

small rooms on the sides. Most rooms have windows opening to each other, but no window opens towards the street/outside. It is surprising to see, how all these buildings are now gone. With so few standing walls, it is difficult to visualise the grandeur of this city.

A mosque and some walls do survive. But it is assumed that these were built during the Mughal era, and not part of the original plan of the fort. Sangin Beg, in his work *Sair-ul-Manazil* mentions, that this mosque was

commissioned by Shaikh Farid, also known as Farid Murtaza Khan, a *bakshee* of Jahangir, after whom the town of Faridabad is named. Farid Murtaza Khan was responsible for several construction projects during the reign of Akbar and Jahangir. However, the dates suggest that the mosque was completed in 1618, two years after the death of Murtaza Khan. Sangin Beg also talks about an inscribed slab on the mosque, which is not there at present time. The slab read: 'Allah is great. In the days of Jahangir Badshah, the younger master Shaikh Farid, who was also known as Murtaza Khan Bukhari, laid the foundation of this mosque. Shaikh Abdullah Ansari finished the construction on 2 Rajab, 1027 Hijri (1618). It was constructed in the honour of Amin-ud-Daulah.'

In one portion of the fort, tall walls with a tiny tank survive. It appears to be the hammam, but without proper documentation, one can only make a visually informed guess.

In Bashir-ud-Din Ahmed's work *Waqiaat-i-Dar-ul Huqumat-i-Delhi*, one can find mention of several underground chambers, which according to him, are 30 to 40 feet deep. Some of them in the royal area are 20 feet wide and have proper ventilation. Due to the depth and ventilation, they also act as 'Sard-Khana' (cold rooms) during summers. There are references to some tunnels also, one of which is near the main tower, connecting Badarpur Road on one side, and runs deep into the other side. Ahmed gives a detailed description of this one. He says that it is pitch dark and has a door within the palace. Due to centuries of neglect, it is dangerous and scary to travel through it. With a small team, he explored the tunnel using lamps and sticks. They travelled some distance and found steps. After climbing 50 steps, they saw a window, from where some light was coming. Continuing further, they exited in the middle of the fort. Ahmed also mentions seven ponds and three *baoli*s within the fort, out of which just two *baoli*s survive today.

Dilapidated stepwell/tank in the citadel

One of these is near the Bijai Mandal, which Ahmed says, was made of granite (sic: Sangkhara). The steps of the *baoli*s and walls have all now collapsed and the tank is filled with wild bushes. He mentions the citadel (royal area) within the city of Tughlaqabad as 'Bala Hisaar'. The main tower is mentioned as 'Sher-Mandal'. In some records, the same tower appears as 'Burj Mandal'. He also mentions that the area under the Bala Hisar may have been populated at some point in time. In his words, 'The fort looks very majestic from outside, but when you enter the gates, all you see are huge piles of stones spread across everywhere, and a small village of Gujjars. This village is popular because people from distant lands come to see the ruins of Tughlaqabad. When one tries to visualize the grandeur of this city, all that comes out of the mouth is 'Allah-hu-Akbar (God is great).'

As we enter the fort, we see a large pit. Ahmed thinks of it as one of the dried ponds, but also records that locals say, that it was a huge hill, which was mined for the stones for this fort. Hence the depression.

On the south-western side, outside the fortified city, a huge lake was constructed, water for which was held with the help of a sluice dam. The dam is now part of the nearby fort of Adilabad, covered in one of the later chapters. An island was created in this lake, which was also fortified in a pentagonal shape and contains a huge tomb. A viaduct connects the island (known as Dar-ul-Aman) with the Fort. The builder of this fort, Sultan Ghias-ud-Din Tughlaq Shah is buried in this fortified tomb, along with his son Sultan Muhammad Bin Tughlaq. In another chamber within the fortification, Ghias-ud-din's

Facing page above: 1924 Archival photo of Tughlaq's Tomb.
Source: ASI Photo Archives

Facing page below: Tomb of Tughlaq, as seen from the fort

The tomb of Ghiasuddin and Muhammad Bin Tughlaq

companion of the Khilji era, General Zafar Khan is buried. Interestingly, we also have a tiny grave in one of the corridors, which is rumoured to be the grave of a dog. For a long period, the underground chambers inside this fortified island were used as a prison. Feroz Shah Tughlaq, in his biographies, mentions that he repaired the structure and added fancy doors

to it. He also mentions that he buried a chest with prayers and blessings of many people at the head of Sultan Muhammad Bin Tughlaq so that he could have a blessed afterlife.

Many historians have noted that Ghias-ud-Din Tughlaq was returning to Delhi in February 1325, when he sent a message to Khwaja Nizamuddin Auliya, that he should move out of the city, or else the Emperor will take care of him when he reaches Delhi. As a reply to that, Khwaja said 'Hunooz Delhi door ast' (Delhi is still far away). As the story goes, the Emperor could not reach Delhi alive from that trip. He had camped in Afghanpur (probably near Moradabad), where his nobles from Delhi, including prince Jauna Khan (later, Mohammad Bin Tughlaq) had built him a temporary palace to halt. All accounts state that the Emperor and his second son, Prince Mahmud Khan, were killed due to collapsing of that structure. Historians, however, differ in how the structure collapsed. Zia-ud-Din Barani (1285–1357) writes that a proper palace was constructed to welcome the King and around noon, he entered the pavilion with proper fanfare. He was supposed to march to Delhi with a much larger celebratory convoy. As they finished lunch, all the nobles stepped out for washing their hands and the Emperor was left alone inside with his favourite son. As mentioned in *Tarikh-i-Firoz Shahi*, at this time, lightning struck the building and the entire pavilion collapsed on the king. Ibn-e-Battuta, in his memoirs, claims that elephants were paraded near this palace and one elephant hit the pavilion causing the damage. However, one must note that Ibn-e-Battuta was not present at the scene. He reached Delhi nine years after the incident. Historians believe that Wazir Khwaja Jahan was responsible for this accident as he conspired and deliberately prepared a weak palace. He was a close ally of prince Jauna Khan and wanted him to become king. Abul Fazl, the prime minister of Emperor Akbar, says that it is not correct to call this accident a conspiracy as the building was prepared in hurry and it was bound to collapse. But again, it was a temporary structure, to be used for just a couple of days. Whatever be the case, the fact is that Emperor Ghias-ud-Din Tughlaq commissioned the most majestic structures till his time and could not survive to even witness its grandeur. Communication between him and Khwaja Nizam-ud-Din Auliya turned out to be Khwaja's prophecies and the Fort got deserted.

Tughlaqabad Plan

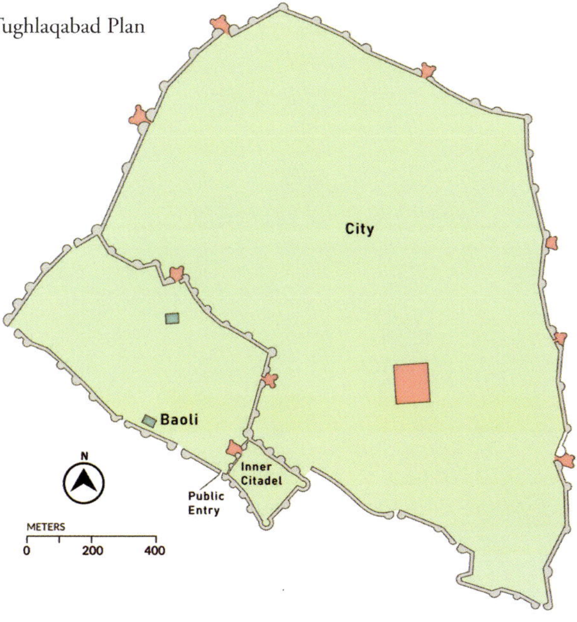

Location	Mehrauli-Badarpur Road
Period	Tughlaq
Public Access	Ticketed
Managing Authority	Archaeological Survey of India
Built by	Ghias-ud-Din Tughlaq Shah
Latitude-Longitude	28.511431481276766, 77.2622858024365

KOTLA-I-FEROZSHAHI

‘Father of the Indian irrigation system’ is one of the many titles that Feroz Shah Tughlaq earned during his reign. Unlike many of his predecessors, his priority was not to expand the kingdom but to provide a better life to those who were under his rule. As a result, he also lost many territories that his cousin and uncle had captured earlier. He was born to Malik Rajab, younger brother of Sultan Ghias-ud-Din Tughlaq, and his wife Bibi Kadbanu, daughter of Rana Mall Bhatti of Abohar. He was orphaned at a young age and spent all his time in the court of his uncle and cousin, learning the affairs of the court. When Muhammad Bin Tughlaq died, Feroz Shah was chosen as the successor by the nobles. But Feroz Shah was reluctant to take the responsibility. He was planning his journey to Mecca and wanted to continue with that, instead of ruling the kingdom. Afif

Facing page: Pyramidal structure with Ashokan Pillar

says that as the long debate and attempt to pursue Feroz Shah was not leading anywhere, Tatar Khan, the head of the delegation, who had come to Thatta to convince Feroz Shah, stood up and held his arm to force him on the throne. He was then presented with the royal robe, which he wore over his robe of mourning and did not let any noble remove that to honour the departed Sultan.

Feroz Shah is known for his numerous constructions of public buildings and irrigation canals. The Tughlaq Dynasty saw 10 rulers in 77 years of their rule. The first three kings ruled for 67 years: Ghias-ud-Din Tughlaq Shah (1321–1325), Muhammad Bin Tughlaq (1325–1351) and Feroz Shah Tughlaq (1351–1388). These three built three different cities and constructed forts. Because of the way Ghias-ud-Din and Muhammad Bin Tughlaq ruled, the Tughlaq dynasty is often considered to be of tyrants and lunatic kings. However, that is not the case. *Tarikh-i-Firoz Shahi*, in the 17th Mukaddama of Kism II, talks about the prosperity in Feroz Shah's kingdom, where contemporary author Shams-i-Siraj Afif says, he reserved 36 lacs of *tanka*s for learned & religious men (spent on education) and 100 lacs of *tanka*s as pension for the poor and

1920 Archival photo of East wall from the river side.
Source: ASI Photo Archives

needy. He was trying to bring equality amongst the population.

Regarding the fort, historians suggest that what remains is just a small part of a much larger complex, within the city of Ferozabad. Neither the extent of the city nor of the palace-fort can be determined with complete accuracy, a lot of destruction has taken place since then.

Afif mentions that to build his city of Ferozabad, the Emperor selected a site, 5 kos (approximately 15 km) away from the city of Delhi. It included places like Kasba of Indrapat, Sarai of Malik Yar Paran, Sarai of Shaikh Abu Bakr Tusi, the village of Gawain, the land of Khetwara, the land of Lahrawat, the land of Andhawali, the land of Sarai of Malika, the land of the tomb of Sultan Raziya, the land of Bhari, the land of Mahrola and the land of Sultanpur. He issued the orders to build this new city before his second visit to Lakhnauti (now Lucknow). To build this city, material from old cities that were in a ruinous state was used. Bashir-ud-Din Ahmed in *Waqiaat-i-Dar-ul Huqumat-i-Delhi* mentions that local travellers with animals were instructed to carry a load of stones while travelling from Delhi (Siri and Mehrauli) to this new city. It took several years, but the task was eventually complete and the forts of Siri, Jahanpanah and Qila Rai Pithora were largely dismantled. He also mentions that from Kasba Indarpat (Purana Qila area) to Kushk-i-Shikaar (Northern Ridge of Delhi), which is 5 kos apart, the entire land was packed with

Inner Gateways of the palace

houses. Roads were flooded with people and not even a small patch of land was left between the buildings. However, when the Emperor came back from his journey, the main buildings of the palace were not complete. Afif mentions in *Tarikh-i-Feroz Shahi* that the emperor stayed in 'Kushk-i-Humayun' temporarily. One may think that Afif is referring to Purana Qila or Humayun's Tomb, but we must remember that the

Mughal Emperor Humayun came to Delhi almost 200 years later. There cannot be any building attributed to him when Afif was writing the book. Hence, he is talking of a building that we no longer identify.

Historians have listed many buildings within the Fort of Ferozabad (Feroz Shah Kotla). Barring three, there is no trace of any other building. While ruins are spread across, it is difficult to identify, which wall belongs to which building. Shams-i-Siraj Afif and later historians who quoted him, mention buildings like Mahal-i-Sahani Geeli (Palace of Clayey Court), Mahal-i-Angur (Palace of Grapes), Mahal-i-Chhajja-i-Chobin (Palace of the Wooden Gallery), Mahal-i-Bar-i-Aam (Palace of the Public Pourt) and Sahni Miyangi (Central Quadrangle), which are not traceable anymore. Zafar Hasan also mentions that the gate where Timur had encamped when he invaded Delhi and where Ibrahim Lodi had set up a bull (brought from Gwalior) is unknown. What survives is a pyramidal structure with Ashokan Pillar on top, the Jami Masjid, *baoli* and ruins of a few other unmarked buildings.

The 18th Mukaddama in Kism III of *Tarikh-i-Firoz Shahi* talks about an invention called Tas-i-Ghariyal,

Interior of the Fort

a clock in which seven different uses of *tas* in marking time and making known the hours of prayer were there. It was installed on the top of the main Darbar and people would often visit the palace just to see it. He mentions that many inventions were installed at the Fort and people were amused by them.

The most interesting part is the outer wall, which, at some locations retain its original height. It has embrasures (arrow slits) near the top but does not have a platform for the soldiers to stand on the inner side. The only speculation one can make is that there must have been a wooden platform on the rear, for the soldiers to walk. But we also do not have any arrangement in the wall where this wooden platform would have been fixed. What is more amusing is the fact, that the slope of these arrow slits is inward. Maulvi Zafar Hasan suggests that it appears, that these slits were designed to fire arrows inside the citadel. This is very unlikely and strange. One may also assume that these are not arrow slits, but vents or shafts kept for light to come in. But that is only required for a closed chamber. These slits are on the wall, where there is no adjoining room/chamber. Another speculation can be that during restoration, these arrow slits were accidentally changed to this arrangement.

The eastern side of the palace is facing towards the river. While Yamuna has now moved over 1 km away, it was flowing right next to Ferozabad, when the city was built. Maulvi Zafar Hasan mentions several staircases leading to the river from the eastern wall, but they no longer exist. Perhaps they were sealed when the monument was restored and converted to a tourist spot.

1920 Archival view of East wall with (now sealed) exit from the river side. *Source: ASI Photo Archives*

Afif mentions that when Feroz Shah was visiting Khizarabad, he crossed Tobra village (now Topra, Yamunanagar, Haryana), where he saw a huge stone column. Another such column was found near Meerut. He says that he read in the work of good historians that these columns were used as the walking sticks and to hurdle cattle by Bheem, the Pandava brother. Emperor Feroz Shah was so much impressed with the pillar that he ordered to source all the available material to facilitate the movement of this obelisk from Tobra to his new city. Parcels of cotton and sembal (silk cotton tree) were spread on the ground around the obelisk, as his men started removing the earth around the pillar. As they cleared the base, the pillar fell on this bed gently with no harm. A square base was discovered at the other end. The obelisk was then covered with reeds and raw skin to save it during transportation.

A carriage with 42 wheels was engineered, with ropes tied to each, pulled by a team of 200 men. Many more men were present to push the carriage, and the Sultan himself was present to observe this task. Several boats were joined together, each with a load-bearing capacity of 5000–7000 mounds of grain. The obelisk was placed on these boats and was transported to Delhi. Afif was 12 years old and an eyewitness in Delhi, when the obelisk was unloaded at the site of Feroz Shah Kotla and kept near Jami Masjid. Several architects were invited to design an appropriate building for the obelisk. They started executing the approved

| The Ashokan Pillar

design stagewise, and with completion of each step, the obelisk was raised to it. Cotton bags and logs of wood were placed all around it, as it was raised a few degrees each day. It was then renamed as Minara-i-Zarin ('Golden Column'). There used to be a golden crown on top of this, which was mentioned by William Flinch in 1611. This pillar, and the other one, which Tughlaq had installed in what we now know as Hindu Rao Hospital of Northern Ridge, are Ashokan Pillars, intact with their original inscriptions. The one at Hindu Rao Hospital was broken into multiple pieces and was restored later.

There are few old paintings of this pyramidal structure, where it is depicted as a regular three-storey building with domed corners and each level slightly smaller in area than the lower one (thus earning its description of a pyramidal structure). The domes are now gone and the staircase only from one side survives, which was restored in 1914. Its chambers, for a long period, were used to worship Djinns, until ASI in 2019, forced all the encroachers out of this monument. Due to oil lamps and incense sticks, the walls of the building were damaged badly. A thick black layer of carbon can be seen on most walls. Such activities are now restricted to

1923 Archival view of the pyramidal structure and Jami Masjid.
Source: ASI Photo Archives

a limited area. On one gate, people put locks on the grill and petition *djinns* to fulfil their desires. Only a few locks can be seen now, and others have been removed.

To the southeast of this pyramidal structure, we have the remains of a square room, which appears to have a corridor around the central hall. Due to a lack of proper records, it is difficult to ascertain the name or purpose of this chamber.

Ruins of a palace north of Jami Masjid

To its south, is the Jami Masjid of Kotla, which has rooms underneath, that must have been used by staff for residential or official purposes. The entrance to the mosque is from the north, with a projected gate with three openings and has steps leading up from two sides. These three openings formerly had carved stonework, which was removed later and added to some building elsewhere. Originally, the mosque was plastered with a lime-based material and had a dazzling whiteness, giving the effect of marble. The

1921 Archival view of the interior of Jami Masjid.
Source: ASI Photo Archives

courtyard of the mosque has a large circle, which originally was a deep pit. Maulvi Zafar Hasan states that it must have been a well originally but was later filled up. In 1914–15, during restoration, an attempt was made to clear the pit and restore it. But as they started digging, they realised that the walls of the pit are too weak to hold the weight and the entire structure might collapse. Hence, it was refilled and sealed forever. In all probability, it was the ablution zone for the people who would come to pray at the mosque.

View of Jami Masjid from the pyramidal structure

In 1793, Capt. W. Francklin of the East India Company mentions a 25 feet high octangular domed roof atop this pit. There also exists a theory that the pillars of this domed *chhatri* were removed to construct the Martello towers in the wall of Shahjahanabad. Timur, in his *Malfuzat* (discourses/memoirs), mentions that he started from Delhi (Mehrauli & Jahanpanah) and marched for 3 kos to reach the fort of Firozabad on the banks of Yamuna. He went inside the Jami Masjid for prayers. Ferishta says that Timur was so much impressed by this architecture that he erected the

View of the stepwell from the pyramidal structure

great mosque at Samarqand modelled on the same. However, when one looks at the Bibi Khanym Mosque (aka Blue Mosque) of Samarqand, it appears to be a replica of the Begumpur Mosque of Delhi, which was also built during the Tughlaq era. It is also recorded

that the great mosque of Samarqand was built by masons taken from Delhi as slaves by Timur.

The mosque is still in use and regular prayers are held there. However, as per the official records of the government, it is abandoned, and no religious activity is supposed to happen.

On the northwest side of the pyramidal structure, we have the only circular *baoli* of Delhi. In the first book of this series, *Delhi Heritage Top 10 Baolis*, this *baoli* of Feroz Shah Kotla is described in great detail. Given its shape, this *baoli* is the largest in Delhi area-wise. It was covered from the top, and probably had an opening in the middle of the roof. There were two *chhatri*s on the east and west sides respectively, which are now gone. Winding staircases beneath both these *chhatri*s take us to the lower arcaded level, which is an underground enclosed pool of water. ASI discovered terracotta pipes leading to the Yamuna, that would help regulate the water level in this *baoli*.

To the north of the *baoli*, there are remains of a small enclosure, which is currently being used by the horticulture department of the Archaeological Survey of India to grow the plants and store gardening essentials, used within this premise.

Famous Belgian priest, Rev. Father Hosten, S.J., who worked elaborately on the antiquities of India in the early 1900s, mention three tunnels under the fort. In his article in the *Journal of the Royal Asiatic Society of Bengal* (vol. 2, no. 4, 1911), he mentions that one of them leads to the river, the other to Kushk-i-Shikar on the ridge, and third to Qila-i-Rai Pithora in Mehrauli. Maulvi Zafar Hasan, in his *Monuments of Delhi* published in 1916, mentions that no such tunnels have been discovered. He is also of a belief that this might be just another local legend. However, in the chapter where Zafar Hasan talks about the *baoli* on the Ridge (now inside the complex of Hindu Rao Hospital), he mentions a tunnel leading to Feroz Shah Kotla. This particular tunnel was originally mentioned by Abul Fazl in his book *Ain-i-Akbari* (1589). British archaeologists cleared the tunnel to some depth, but then came back and sealed it permanently.

While travelling through the palace, the most interesting element that one can observe is that several visitors come to this place with religious intentions. One can often see Buddhist pilgrims, standing atop the pyramidal structure, praying in front of the Ashokan Pillar. Since the pillar bears an inscription, giving Ashoka's message to accept Buddhism, pilgrims from Southeast Asia often visit this place, along with Ashokan Pillar on ridge and Ashokan rock edict in East of Kailash (near Iskcon Temple, Delhi) for prayers. From here, they continue their journey to other Buddhist sites like Gaya and Sarnath.

Right under the pillar, in the arcaded corridors of the pyramidal structure, and the rooms under the Jami Masjid, one can spot Muslims and Hindus sitting with some wizard/oracle, who claims to have controlled a *djinn* and can help them with their problems. Feroz Shah Kotla is said to be the abode of *djinn*s and is very popular amongst locals, who believe in the concept. The 'Surah al-Jinn' in Quran talks about the concept of *djinn*s, and how they are made out of the smokeless fire. They are descendants of Satan and inherit satanic powers. If one can impress a *djinn*, he can get anything done from it. Therefore, people started flocking to Feroz Shah Kotla, when the word

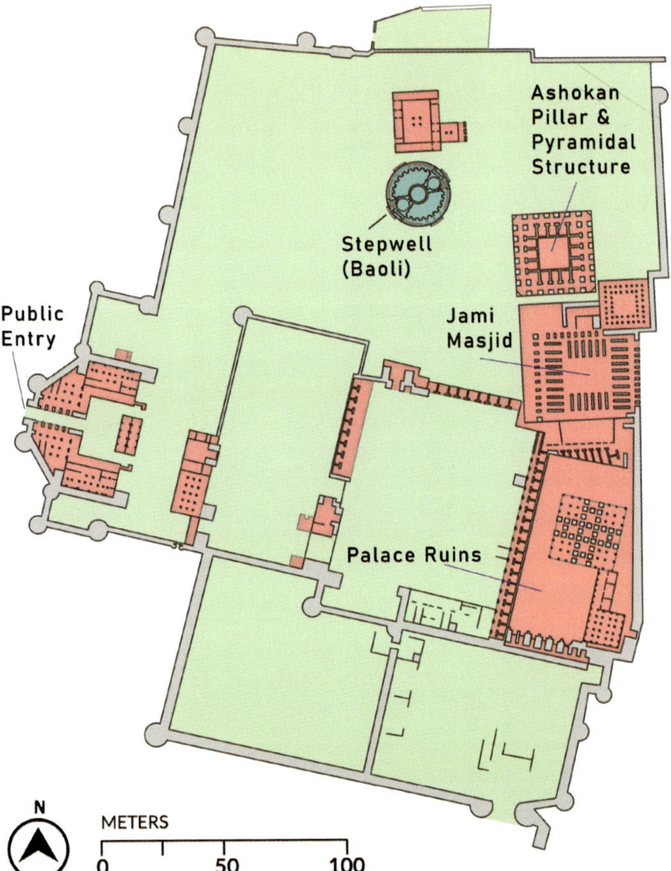

| Feroz Shah Kotla Plan

spread that this palace is possessed by these invisible creatures. There was a time when every alcove and arch of Kotla started turning black due to smoke coming out of oil lamps, that people would put. A thick layer of carbon covered many walls and it was so sticky, that people started sticking coins as offerings and petitions on them. In 2019, the ASI started its efforts to stop all such illegal activities. These self-proclaimed black magicians were not only harming the heritage but also scamming innocent people. As of now, only a small portion of the fort is made available to the worshippers. Instead of oil lamps, incense sticks are used. People had put several padlocks on the gates as one form of prayer, a few of which is still there and no new locks are being put.

Location	Behind Feroz Shah Kotla Stadium
Period	Tughlaq
Public Access	Ticketed
Managing Authority	Archaeological Survey of India
Built by	Feroz Shah Tughlaq
Latitude-Longitude	28.63497878150344, 77.24275085605076

SALIMGARH

NOORGARH

Jalal Khan, the second son of Sher Shah Suri, took over after him and assumed the regnal name Islam Shah Suri in 1545 CE. His reign was the longest in the Suri Dynasty, spanning more than eight years and was succeeded by five kings, who could only propel the empire for two years. This was the time when Humayun had become powerful once again and taken over areas like Kabul and Kandahar from his half-brother Kamran Mirza. Islam Shah had helped his father in deposing Humayun from Hindustan and now feared that the latter was on his way to reclaim his throne with a powerful army. Islam Shah started strengthening the city's defences. In one such attempt, he identified a tiny island protected by river Yamuna, outside the gates of his city, to the northern side. Yamuna was flowing on the right side but had a small tributary going from the left, making it a riverine

| Corridor of the jail

Entry to Salimgarh from Red Fort

island. It was not possible to reach this island on foot. Islam Shah, who is also known as Saleem Shah Suri, realised that this island can be a strong outpost. He built a fort on it, which came to be known as Salimgarh.

Tarikh-i-Dawudi mentions that when Islam Shah Suri heard of Humayun returning from Persia, he marched from Lahore and came to Delhi. He then commissioned a fort in the middle of the Yamuna. He wanted to make the strongest fort and succeeded to some extent. The fort appears to be carved out of a single stone.

Maulvi Zafar Hasan notes that Salimgarh is a polygonal-shaped fort, built with solid rubble masonry walls, and contains several bastions. Only the walls were completed during the lifetime of Salim Shah Suri and the work halted with his death in 1546. Later, the possession of the fort was granted by Emperor Akbar to Farid Murtaza Khan Bukhari. Farid Murtaza Khan held high ranks during the reign of Akbar and Jahangir. He was in charge of several buildings along the Badshahi Sadak (later called G.T. Road) and was given the land, which he named after him as Faridabad. He was a man of high influence and power in the early Mughal era.

Zafar Hasan notes that Murtaza Khan held extensive possessions along with banks of River Yamuna. Bashir-ud-Din Ahmed, in *Waqiaat-i-Dar-ul Huqumat-i-Delhi* also mentions Murtaza Khan as an important figure. He states that five years before the death of Salim Shah Suri, the fort was started but by the time of his death, only the outer wall was built at the expense of 4 lakh of rupees. 18 years later, Murtaza Khan received this fort as *jagir*. He built many buildings inside this. But by 1828, all of these buildings, except one or two, were destroyed. One garden, however, was maintained, which was used by Emperor Akbar Shah II.

Sir Syed Ahmed Khan mentions that during the tenure of Jahangir (1621), a strong bridge was built on the Yamuna to reach the fort. That bridge was incorporated into the plan of Red Fort and appears to be an integral part of the Red Fort. The bridge was present during the time of Ahmed. It was during the era of Badshah Nooruddin Jahangir, that this fort came to be known as Noorgarh. However, it did retain its original name 'Salimgarh' in common parlance.

A gate was later added by emperor Bahadur Shah, which contained a slab, bearing the following inscription:

> Line 1: 'When, by the grace of God, this gate, which is beautiful and augmentative of happiness, was built,'
>
> Line 2: 'Knowledge spoke the year of its erection, O Zafar; The door magnificent as heaven and of auspicious foundation.'

Maulvi Zafar Hasan notes the date of this inscription as 1854-55 CE, which gives the date of construction of this gate. He also notes that the marble slab with

The railway bridge; on left is Red Fort and on right Salimgarh

the inscription was removed and kept in the museum when the bridge was demolished to make way for the new railway bridge. The original gate, which led to the Yamuna and the bridge of boats, was sealed. Impression of its arch can still be seen from the outside, where the road has been raised to a level, that the gate is half-buried in it. From the inside, the original Salimgarh gate and its ramp to the Yamuna still exists.

Hasan also notes that the mosque inside the fort is of rubble masonry and contains three compartments.

Above: Remains of the mosque

Facing page above: Original Salimgarh Darwaza of Red Fort

Facing page below: Present Salimgarh gate, built by the British

The central apartment is covered by a late Pathan dome, while the remaining ones have vaulted roofs. The 'Pathan' era refers to the Suri dynasty, which means, the mosque was built during the time of Islam Shah Suri. He mentions that the south chamber is under military occupation.

When the city of Shahjahanabad was planned, the fort of Salimgarh was very smartly incorporated into it. A gate from the Red Fort opened to the bridge of Jahangir, that took you straight to Salimgarh. Since the fort was on an island, it was secluded from the outer world and the only way, besides a boat, was through the bridge. It made Salimgarh of utmost strategic importance. During the reign of Aurangzeb, the fort was converted to a prison for some elite prisoners. The emperor confined his own daughter, Zeb-un-Nisa, in this fort for 20 years, till her death. Later, Princes Murad Baksh and Sulaiman Shikoh were also incarcerated here before they were taken to the Gwalior Fort.

In 1788, Ghulam Qadir Rohilla was trying to locate the Mughal treasure but found nothing. Drunk Qadir got so angry that he pierced the eyes of Emperor Shah Alam II on 10 August. For about 20 days, the Mughal family was facing their worst time at the hands of their Wazir, Ghulam Qadir. Mughal princesses were stripped naked and made to dance in front of him. They eventually committed suicide by jumping into River Yamuna. These acts of Qadir turned all his allies against him. To protect the Mughal royal family, Mahadji Shinde, the Maratha king of Gwalior came to Delhi. Ghulam Qadir used Salimgarh to escape through the Yamuna but was caught by the

Marathas, who eventually punished him for his inhumane atrocities.

During the reign of Emperor Akbar Shah II, this fort was converted to a place of retirement, where the emperor would come and stay undisturbed by the public.

The last Mughal emperor, Bahadur Shah Zafar used this fort during the rebellion of 1857. He would hold meetings here and discuss battle strategy. When the British were about to re-enter Delhi with full force, and most of the rebels were removed, Bahadur Shah left this fort and headed to Humayun's Tomb, where he was ultimately captured. The British then brought the emperor to Salimgarh and kept him here, until he was shifted to Rangoon, where he died.

In 1864, the British started laying the tracks for the East Indian Railway line. It connected Calcutta with Delhi and opened a new trade channel. The tracks were laid right through the Salimgarh fort, dividing it into two parts. To achieve this, the British also removed the old bridge built by Jahangir and constructed two new bridges, one for road traffic and the other for the railway line. Given the alignment of the railway line, British engineers had to chip off a corner of the Red Fort. The wall was then sealed with a separate material, which is still distinguished easily. They also constructed a long iron bridge to the east side of the Fort, connecting the two ends of the river. Bashir-ud-Din notes that the (iron) bridge starts 953 miles from Calcutta and is 2649 feet long. It was completed in 1867 and set upon to public transport. This is a double-decked

truss bridge. This bridge and line are still functional. The upper deck is a double-line railway track while the lower level is a four-lane road.

In 1945, after the fall of Japan, the British Army captured several soldiers of the Indian National Army, including Gen. Mohan Singh, GoC of the first INA, and the three Generals of Netaji's INA, Colonel Prem Sahgal, Colonel Gurbaksh Singh Dhillon and

The two bridges built by the British. On left is the railway bridge and on right is for foot/carriage traffic

Jail in front with 2 barracks visible behind it

Major General Shah Nawaz Khan. Some of these were kept in the stepwell of Red Fort. Many of these were brought to Salimgarh Fort and a makeshift prison was constructed for them. The prison still stands as a testimony to the period. In the walls of the Red Fort, the INA trials started, in which the first case of the three generals of Netaji's INA was being heard. These trials are famous as the 'Red Fort Trials'. There was a popular cry during those days: 'Laal Qile se aayi awaaz, Sehgal, Dhillon, Shahnawaz' ('A cry came from Red Fort, Sehgal, Dhillon & Shahnawaz').

Top: Interior of the jail cell

Above left: Smaller room inside the jail

Above right: Corridor of the jail

A British barrack

Since 1857, the Salimgarh Fort was occupied by the army. After Independence, the Indian Army continued to stay there. In 1992, this led to several complications with the UNESCO World Heritage Site listing as there were multiple stakeholders. The Archaeological Survey of India had to file a petition in the court to gain possession. In 2003, a major portion of the fort was vacated, and the restoration began. About 8 million rupees were spent on the Salimgarh Fort restorations before the commonwealth games of 2010. A museum was also set up, housing the memories of the Indian National Army, along with the belongings of Dhillon, Sehgal and Khan.

The fort is still divided by the railway line. The northern area is accessible via a bridge, where visitors can see the old mosque, museums, barracks, and the jail. The southern side contains the barracks of the Central Industrial Security Force (CISF), the unit that is responsible for the protection of the fort. Since 2019, due to restoration activities, the entry to Salimgarh Fort is closed for tourists.

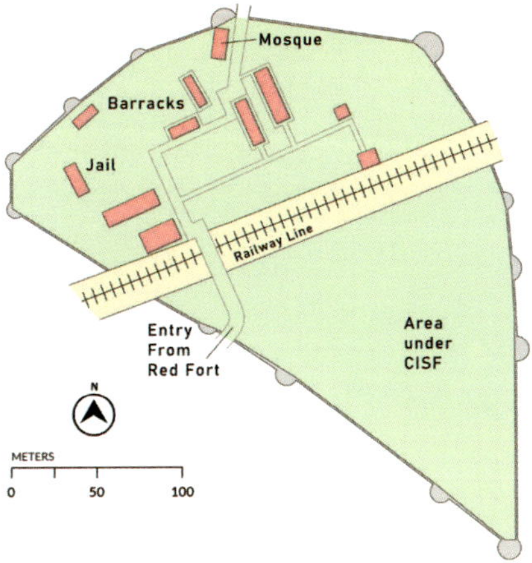

Salimgarh Plan

Location	Behind Red Fort
Period	Afghan
Public Access	Restricted (Through Red Fort)
Managing Authority	Archaeological Survey of India and Central Industrial Security Force (CISF)
Built by	Islam Shah Suri
Latitude-Longitude	28.660489519367264, 77.2422264782111

LAL KOT & QILA-I-RAI PITHORA

Intersection of the walls of Qila Rai Pithora and Jahanpanah

The origin of Delhi has several stories associated with it. Some are regarded as myths and some as legends. Numerous archaeological evidences suggest that Delhi is thousands of years old and like any other civilisation, the city was built over and over, adding several layers of history. Towns were deserted one after another until Anangpal Tomar came to settle the area now famous as Mehrauli in the 7th century. Since then, we have had an unbroken chain. Later in the 11th century, his successor Anangpal II, also known as Anekpal Tomar, built a tank known as Anangtal and a fort known as Lal Kot (Lit: Red Fortress).

Lal Kot became a matter of debate amongst archaeologists and historians. Its structure, use, location and extent remained a mystery. In the mid-1860s and 1870s, when the British archaeologists were preparing their reports on Delhi's monuments, the debate over Lal Kot started. Major General Alexander Cunningham suggested that we do not know the exact location of Lal Kot. The wall that we see beyond Adham Khan's tomb is part of Qila-i-Rai Pithora, the fort of Prithviraj Chauhan. Also, the wall, which people then believed to be Lal Kot had a different material at some places, which showed that

Archival view of Lal Kot with Adham Khan's tomb visible in background. *Source: ASI Photo Archives*

some portion was built/repaired during the Khilji period. To this, J. D. Begler mentioned a trace of the wall that was visible from the top of Qutub Minar. Upon closer inspection, they found out that this wall connects two points in the other wall (believed to be of Qila-i-Rai Pithora) and is much older than the latter. The masonry was different, suggesting that these were the true remains of Lal Kot. Carr Stephen was a British officer, who documented the history and archaeological remains in India. He mentioned in his work, that Lal Kot was a residential palace, built out of red sandstone. His theory was based on a certain local tradition. Later historians like Bashir-ud-Din Ahmed also believe that the actual location of Lal Kot is unknown. His work was published in 1919, much after the reports of all major British archaeologists from Cunningham to Zafar Hasan.

In this context, the work of Sir Syed Ahmed Khan adds more confusion. In *Asar-us-Sanadid*, Sir Syed mentions that the wall of Qila-i-Rai Pithora, the fort of Prithvi Raj Chauhan has been dated to 1143 CE. However, Prithviraj was not even born at that time. Prithviraj Chauhan was born in 1149 and took over Delhi from his maternal grandfather, Raja Anangpal III (also known as Arkpal, Dakatpal or Mukundpal

Archival view of Lal Kot wall with Qutub Minar visible in background. *Source: ASI Photo Archives*

Tomar) in 1180, thus ending the four-century long Tomar Empire. His rule continued till 1192 until Mohammad of Ghor defeated him in the Battle of Tarain (now called Taraori). He is known to have built a strong fortification around Delhi to defend it from invasions. This fortification became popular with its Persian name 'Qila-i-Rai Pithora'. Rai Pithora is the traditional name of Prithvi Raj Chauhan. If we believe the date given by Sir Syed, then the fort must have been built by Raja Mahipal Singh Tomar (reigned: 1105–1151), who is also the settler of the area now known as Mahipalpur (near Delhi International Airport). Maj. General Cunningham has calculated the date of construction of Qila-i-Rai Pithora to be between 1180 and 1186, which fits the period of Prithviraj Chauhan.

A lot of research and excavations have been happening in this area. The Archaeological Survey of India today demarcates the two forts, based on the reports by J.D. Begler and Maulvi Zafar Hasan. Lal Kot is believed to be in Sanjay Van, the area sandwiched between Mehrauli, Jawaharlal Nehru University and Lado Sarai. The fort wall runs from the Tomb of Adham Khan (locally popular as Bhool Bhulaiyya), opposite the Mehrauli bus terminal, and goes northwards. It takes a turn near the shrine of Ashiq Allah in Sanjay

Remains of the bastion of Lal Kot

Van towards north-east and a little ahead, turns to the east. A little further, it turns back south, but vanishes shortly after, at the Sohan gate. Archaeologists could find the traces of old walls from this point onwards, which must have got damaged with time. The remains continue towards Yogmaya temple and connect back to the wall near Adham Khan's tomb. This missing piece of wall was pointed by Begler, the outline of which he saw from the top of Qutub Minar and further analysed. It was this portion of the wall that had the older material and gave a hint that the continuation we just mentioned, is the original Lal Kot. However, this would put the major water source of the city, the Anangtal, outside the walls. Sir Alexander Cunningham had raised this point that how come the king would leave the major source of water outside the fort walls, prey to enemies in the event of an attack. Other archaeologists believed that the wall did not turn south from the Sohan gate. Instead, it continued to take a full circle around the present Qutub Minar Complex and Quli Khan's tomb (Mehrauli Archaeological Park), to meet the wall starting at Adham Khan's tomb.

To its east, Prithviraj Chauhan made his extension. It is difficult to find the exact spot from where his extension branched out. A large portion of this wall is now gone. But archaeologists believe that it started from Fateh Burj. The remaining portion starts from the Qutub Golf Course on the intersection on Aurobindo Marg (formerly Delhi-Qutub Road), from where the road turns towards Saket (Press Enclave Marg). The crossing appears on maps as PTS Chowk. The old wall of Qila-i-Rai Pithora can be seen on that corner, running towards the east, along with walls of the Qutub Golf Course. Where the golf course ends, we have a large park, named Rai Pithora Cultural Complex. This park also has a modern circular building that earlier functioned as a museum and later housed a library. It was cleared some time ago

Statue of Prithvi Raj Chauhan in Rai Pithora Cultural Complex

for repairs and is currently locked. On the top of this building, there is a statue of Prithvi Raj Chauhan on a horse, installed by the government authorities. It is in this park, that we can see the intersection of the walls of Qila-i-Rai Pithora of Prithvi Raj Chauhan and that of Jahanpanah, the city of Mohammad Bin Tughlaq. The tiny piece of the wall of Jahanpanah inside this park is the only remaining portion of that city. From this intersection, the wall of Qila-i-Rai Pithora turns south and continues until it crosses the Mehrauli–Badarpur Road. After intersecting the road, it turns slightly towards the South–West and continues for about 700 metres. Then it turns towards north-west and continues till the Mehrauli–Gurgaon (MG) Road. The wall disappears at this intersection. However, just by looking at it, one can assume that crossing the present-day Mehrauli Archaeological Park, the wall must have met the wall of Lal Kot near the tomb of Adham Khan. It is interesting to see that the area covered by Lal Kot and Qila-i-Rai Pithora got completely deserted, while people inhabited the areas outside the walls. Other than the Lado Sarai colony and the Christian Colony (Mehrauli), we do not find a dense settlement within the walls. The areas that fall inside the walls are Mehrauli Archaeological Park, Qutub Complex, Qutub Golf Course, Rai Pithora

Cultural Complex, Sanjay Van and a large piece of land between Ahimsa Sthal and Said-ul-Ajab village.

Given the dispute over the exact shape of Lal Kot, it is difficult to be sure of its exact size. However, combined with Qila-i-Rai Pithora, it is safe to say that the wall must have been 6–7 km long. A large portion of it is damaged. The remaining wall in Sanjay Van (marked as Lal Kot) is 1.4 km long and the remaining wall covering Qutub Golf Course & Lado Sarai (marked as Qila-i-Rai Pithora) is a little less than 2.5 km. The wall had a ditch around it, which varied from 18 to 35 feet. It is all filled up now. Wall was 60 feet high and 30 feet thick at most places; however, a large portion of this is dilapidated.

No original building from inside the fort survives today. One may contest that the remains found inside the Qutub Minar Complex are from this era, but we are not sure of the location of those structures. Hence, we cannot ascertain the exact location (inside or outside the fort), from where the stones for Quwwat-ul-Islam were procured.

One thing that we need to keep in mind is that the concept of 'true arch' was not prevalent during the

A gate of Lal Kot, with the grave of Haji Rozbih

era of Lal Kot and Qila-i-Rai Pithora. With trabeated and corbelled arches, it is difficult to construct a huge gateway. Hence, one can observe the unique style of gateways in older forts. They are not covered from the top. Rather, they create several obstacles for the incoming troupes by building strong walls and

complex entrances. For example, in the case of Ranjit Gate of Lal Kot, one would enter through a narrow passage from North to South. After a few feet, taking a U-turn around the high wall, one would start walking towards the north and a little ahead, through a small opening in the wall, would turn towards East. Then he would encounter a large moat and walk around the moat, he would enter the main bastion from West to East. Just a few feet away, he would face another high wall and had to go around it to reach a much thicker wall, with a small opening, that would take this person inside the Lal Kot. But not all gates were this complex. Badaun Gate and Sohan Gate were much simpler and smaller but must have had different implementations of security.

A large portion of the wall, as well as gates, were repaired over and over. Gates of Lal Kot identified by the British Archaeologists were Ranjit Gate (Near Dargah of Ashiq Allah in Sanjay Van), Fateh Burj (where the grave of Haji Rozbih is situated), Sohan Gate, Ghazni Gate (near Adham Khan's Tomb). Those of Qila-i-Rai Pithora were Badaun Gate, Hauz Rani Gate and Barka Gate. While it appears to have a few more gates, but their names are not known.

These forts appear in the writings of a few Muhammadan writers. Ibn-i-Batutta describes Badaun Gate as the 'big gate' and it appears to be the principal entrance of the city during the Muhammadan rule. Amir Khusrow, who was employed by Emperor Balban and later served his successors, before becoming a disciple of Khwaja Nizamuddin also writes of this city and talks of its 13 gates. Amir Timur Gurkani (Taimur/Tamerlane) however mentions only 10 gates that he saw when he invaded Delhi in 1398. General Cunningham also believed that there were 10 gates in total, however, few of those 10 are still to be traced. One of the later period gates is Chaumukha Darwaza, situated in Mehrauli Archaeological Park, near the wall of the Qutub Complex. It is in the least visited area of the park. The gate has proper arches and one can also see the use of leftover stones from a temple. This shows that this is the work of later period Muhammadan rulers.

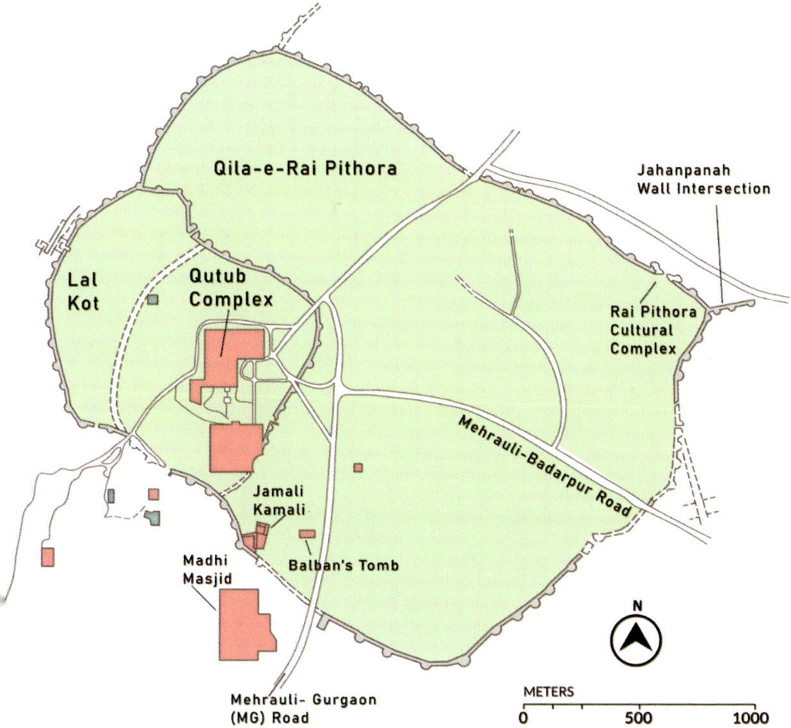

Qila-i-Rai Pithora Plan

Location	Mehrauli and Lado Sarai
Period	Rajput
Public Access	Free Entry
Managing Authority	Archaeological Survey of India
Built by	Anangpal Tomar and Prithvi Raj Chauhan
Latitude-Longitude	Lal Kot: 28.52971623023331, 77.18357795216693 Qila Rai Pithora: 28.528499834840947, 77.20234553167788

ADILABAD

MUHAMMADABAD OR HAZAR SUTOON

'Your arrival is blessed; be at ease, I shall be compassionate to you and give you such favours that your fellow-countrymen will hear of it and come to join you,' said Sultan Muhammad Adil Tughlaq Shah, more commonly known as Muhammad Bin Tughlaq, to Moroccan traveller Ibn Battuta, when the latter met him. As per Battuta's records, the emperor returned from one of his trips on 8 June 1334 and met him for the first time in his palace, which we now know as Adilabad.

The fort of Adilabad is situated opposite the majestic fortified city of Tughlaqabad. Sir Syed states that this fort was built by Muhammad Bin Tughlaq in 1327 and thus earned the name Muhammadabad. Tughlaq was coronated as Muhammad Adil Tughlaq Shah, hence the fort is also known as Adilabad.

Previous page: Present entry into the Adilabad Fort

He also mentions that the palace had 1000 white marble pillars, which gave it the title of 'Hazaar Sutoon' ('Thousand Pillars'). Bashir-ud-Din Ahmed writes that since the fort is very small, it is highly unlikely that it had a thousand pillars. Today, no building inside the fort survives. Originally, it had one or more double-storeyed structures inside it. But Ahmed says that there must be some Baradari (12 arched pavilions) with two levels. He does mention that this building, which was called 'Hazar Sutoon', was different from another building by the same name, built by Alauddin Khilji. The Hazar Sutoon of Khilji became part of the city of Jahanpanah. Interestingly, we have a palace named Qasr-i-Hazaar Sutoon (literally 'Palace of Thousand Pillars'), opposite Sarvpriya Vihar Club in Malviya Nagar, Delhi. It is more commonly known as Bijai Mandal and is believed to be the palace of Muhammad Bin Tughlaq. This building also seems to be different from Alaudin Khilji's Hazaar Sutoon. Ibn Battuta, who was an eyewitness to the grandeur of this fort, mentions that there is a large hall, which has several pillars and roofs layered with lime plaster and very rich looking paintwork. He does not mention any marble or even 1000 pillars. In present times, traces of a hall and some chambers do remain.

Bashir-ud-Din Ahmed also writes that some historians believe, that Ghias-ud-Din Tughlaq Shah died in this palace, which is completely wrong. Ghias-ud-Din died in a makeshift pavilion several kilometres away from Delhi, near a village called Afghanpur.

Interior of the Adilabad Fort

Writers like Bashir-ud-Din Ahmed have linked the fort of Adilabad to Nai ka Kot, another nearby fort (described in a later chapter in this book). Ahmed writes that Adilabad Fort was for the emperor, while the army used to garrison in the adjoining smaller fort, Nai ka Kot. In both these fortifications, at the Bala Hisar, there are important buildings. In Persian, '*Bala*' means high and '*Hisar*' means fort. However, in this context, Bala Hisar means the highest point in the fort.

Inner fortification, with outer fortification visible

Sir Syed Ahmed Khan considers this fort to be the retreat of the Emperor, while the main palace was Jahanpanah's Bijai Mandal. Some historians developed a belief that Adilabad was the citadel of the city of Jahanpanah, built by Muhammad Bin

Tughlaq. However, it is unlikely that this fort was connected to the city walls, as the Jahanpanah wall connected Qila Rai Pithora to Siri, and is several kilometres away from this place.

This is a small fort with a wall, less than 900 metres long, covering an area of 0.02 sq. km only. It is situated on a hill near the lake towards the south of Tughlaqabad. On another hill, we have a small fortification, which contains the huge iconic tomb of Ghiasuddin and Muhammad Bin Tughlaq. Some historians believe that Ghiasuddin built his tomb during his lifetime, but others say that Muhammad Bin Tughlaq built that along with Adilabad, after his father died. The north wall of Adilabad was facing the large lake and on the southern and eastern side, it had a second peripheral wall, which becomes a causeway, connecting the Tughlaqabad Fort. This causeway has a few sluice gates, acting as a dam for the lake. This

wall, starting from the Western gate of the fort and covering the entire south and east sides is roughly 1.25 km long. While the original lake that covered this fort was huge, a few decades ago a small pond was developed towards the north of this fort, in an attempt to revive a part of the original waterbody. The small pond, commonly known as the Tughlaqabad Pond, connected to Kaya Maya Park, sometimes becomes dry and wet depending on the season.

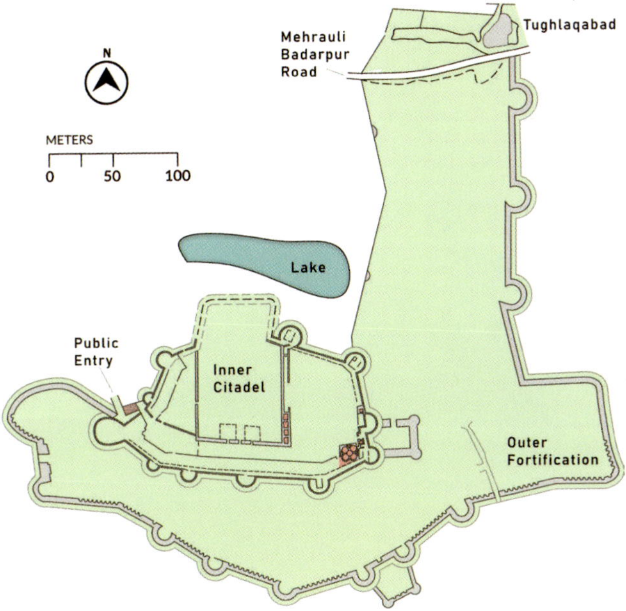

Adilabad Plan

Facing page: Second gate of Adilabad Fort

Location	Opposite Tughlaqabad Fort
Period	Tughlaq
Public Access	Free Entry
Managing Authority	Archaeological Survey of India
Built by	Muhammad Bin Tughlaq (aka Muhammad Adil Tughlaq Shah)
Latitude-Longitude	28.505519099218915, 77.2665049805482

SIRI FORT

In 1296, an 11-year-old boy was witness to a strange change of events, where the most powerful Khalji general, Ali Gurshasp, invited his uncle, Sultan Jalal-ud-Din Feroz Khalji, to talk. While the Sultan embraced his nephew, forgiving all his mistakes, the nephew had his uncle assassinated in a very unmerciful way. The Sultan's head was paraded in multiple cities to strike the fear of this general, who was now coronated as Sultan Ala-ud-din Khalji.

That 11-year-old boy lived till the time of Sultan Feroz Shah Tughlaq and wrote the story of the Delhi Sultanate from the period of Sultan Ghias-ud-Din Balban to whatever time he saw of Feroz Shah Tughlaq. His book was compiled as *Tarikh-i-Firoz Shahi* and is considered to be the most authentic eyewitness of the time. This boy was Zia-ud-din Barani. After

Previous page: Remains of the wall of Siri

Ala-ud-Din Khilji took over Delhi, Barani's father and uncle were given respectable positions in the government. Barani not only saw the affairs as an outsider, but he was also an audience to family discussions, where the brothers would be deliberate about their assignments. Later, during the Tughlaq era, Barani was appointed as the *Nadim* (companion) of Muhammad bin Tughlaq.

Barani in his book mentions that people were not only upset with Ala-ud-Din Khalji but also called his actions unholy and barbaric. However, Ala-ud-Din, during his march to Delhi showered gold coins in every village. As a result, by the time he reached the River Yamuna, he had a large following and his army was stronger than ever. A puppet king who had been installed in Delhi fled to Multan as Ala-ud-Din was preparing to cross the River Yamuna. Barani mentions that upon crossing the river, Ala-ud-Din came to a village called Siri and from here, marched to Delhi (Mehrauli/Qila-i-Rai Pithora).

Barani, in the next pages of his book, gives a detailed account of the atrocities of the new emperor. He also talks about how the learned men got upset with him, especially because of his inhumane ways to crush any

1920 Archival view of one of the bastions of Siri Wall, that now marks the entry of Shahpur Jat village.
Source: ASI Photo Archives

opposition that he faced. Khalji was busy with his conquests when Mughals (read: Mongols) realised that Delhi is defenceless. While Khalji was attacking Chittorgarh, Targhi Beg advanced towards Delhi. After finishing up in Chittorgarh, Khalji returned to Delhi quickly to save it from Targhi. The battle of Chittor had made his army very weak. His journey to Delhi was interfered with heavy rains. They somehow made it to the city in time, but the army was in no position to fight. Sultan himself camped far from the capital, at the ground of Siri, while Targhi had seized all roads leading to the capital of Delhi (the area around Mehrauli). Sultan's little remaining army started building entrenchments and defence in Siri village and prepared for the battle. Barani writes that since the supply was stopped, people were under great fear and were preparing to leave the capital. Mughals slowly started taking over nearby villages and also plundered royal stores at many places. They started selling grain and other looted articles at a much cheaper cost. Barani writes that the entire Mughal army got busy drinking wine and while they had few skirmishes with the army of Sultan, neither party could win. Targhi Beg and his Mughal army had a clear advantage and morally, the people of Delhi, as well as Sultan's army, had prepared to accept a defeat, and perhaps a painful death. However, after two months of plundering and drinking wine, the Mughals all of a sudden return. Barani mentions that if the Mughals would have stayed another month, the supply at the capital would have exhausted and the capital would have fallen automatically. But the enemy could not hold it longer and had to return.

Barani appears to be heavily surprised with how the battle turned around. He mentions that Sultan Ala-ud-Din Khilji woke from his sleep of neglect after this incident. He had been busy expanding his empire and conquering forts, while his capital was always left exposed to the invaders. Hence, he decided to build a new capital with a much stronger fortification. The land he chose for this task was the ground of the village of Siri, where he built an oval city. Eventually, the new fort became popular with the name 'Siri Fort'. While the new fort was being built, he also repaired the existing wall of capital (Lal Kot and Qila-i-Rai Pithora). This explains certain elements in Purana Qila, which do not appear to be of Rajput style.

The most common story associated with Siri Fort has been that after Ala-ud-Din Khalji built his new capital (Dar-ul-Khilafat), people from Mongolia attacked it and the Khalji army was able to defeat them. Around 8000 enemies were slain and their severed heads were hung on the wall of this capital, thus giving it the name 'Siri' (In Hindi, the head is known as *sir or siri*). However, no historic document talks of the connection of this name. Given the accounts of Sir Alexander Cunningham, Ibn Battuta, Zia-ud-Din Barani and many more, it is evident that the name Siri predates the era of Ala-ud-Din Khalji. But Sir Syed Ahmed Khan, in his work *Asar-us-Sanadid*, do mention that while the fort wall was nearing completion, 8000 Mughal heads were brought here and added to the wall while raising the masonry higher. In the footnote, Sir Syed mentions of *Tarikh-i-Alai*. This story does not find mention in Barani's work, who took special care of writing about almost every battle of Khalji and how the enemies were slain over and over. Barani writes that after building the new capital, Sultan also commissioned several forts around Delhi to have better protection. Mughals continued to attack and every time, they would be defeated and taken as prisoners. Their severed heads would be stacked on each other to create a tower. He writes that even today, a tall tower of skulls stands outside the Budayun Gate (of Qila-i-Rai Pithora), a testament to the power of Ala-ud-Din Khalji. He does not mention any head being added to the wall of Siri Fort. Barani says that every time, the army of Islam was victorious, and the Mughals were defeated. One time, several thousand Mughals were taken prisoners and kept in the fort of Naraina. Their wives and kids were brought to the capital and sold away. A unit of the army was sent to Naraina to execute every prisoner and streams ran with the foul blood of Mughals. It should be noted here that the fort of Naraina finds mention in a few other records too. During the British era, they recorded that just a few pillars of the original fort survived. As of today, even those are gone. The fort was on some hill in Naraina. That belt is now a busy industrial zone of Delhi.

Coming back to Ala-ud-Din Khalji, Barani mentions that Khalji defeated Mughals so many times, that they gave up on the dream of capturing Hindustan and accepted the might of Islam. It must be mentioned here that Ghenghis Khan (also called Changez Khan) followed the Tengrism religion. His son Chagatai Khan continued with the same. One of Genghis' grandsons, Berke Khan converted to Islam in 1252. However, the Chagatai Khanate that attacked Delhi had not yet converted to Islam. After several defeats, many of the Chagatai Mongol/Mughal soldiers converted to Islam under Khalji's banner. These people, amongst other converts of India, were mentioned as 'New Musalmans' by Barani. There was also an incident where the 'New Musalmans' revolted against the Sultan and the rebellion was crushed in Khalji's merciless style. Barani notes that all these Musalmans were killed and their families punished in an equally brutal way. Towards the end of the reign of Khalji, a handful of 'New Musalmans' were vocal about their poverty and ill-treatment by the Sultan. There was a faded rumour of a revolt. Barani writes that Sultan heard this chatter and got so angry, that he ordered that every 'New Musalman' around his capital should be killed. About 30,000 people were slaughtered around Siri Fort, most of them having no knowledge of why the Sultan issued such orders.

Talking of the new fortified city built by Ala-ud-Din Khalji, Maulvi Zafar Hasan mentions that the lost city of Siri was surrounded by a rubble fortification, with seven gates. Traces of walls are present at some places and the village is now known as Shahpur Jat, notes Zafar. He adds that monuments within the village were built at a later date, and no original building from inside the fort survives. He does mention a bastion and ruins of a gateway in the South-East corner, and a small portion of 8 feet wide wall, remaining on the western side. These western ruins remain till date and are now under the protection of the Archaeological Survey of India. At one point, it is a double-wall, with a narrow passage within, running from Siri Fort Auditorium to the entry of Shahpur Jat village. A little portion of the wall towards the south side (Panchsheel Park North) and to North-West (narrow green patch between Siri Fort Sports Complex and Gargi college) remains. The one outside the Siri Fort Complex (North-East of Fort) has been restored, but not to its original height. One can see the thickness of the wall and the bastions. A beautiful mosque, called Muhammadiwali is also situated along this wall. Being from a much later period (Lodhi era), it shows that for a long time, this area remained populated. Another mosque, recorded as Bulbulki is supposed to be on the other side of this wall, however, it is long gone, and the mentioned location now falls inside Siri Fort Sports Complex.

Zafar Hasan also notes that this fort of Siri was destroyed by Sher Shah Suri, who used the material for his new city, which became popular as Dilli Sher Shahi. Later the material from that city's walls was

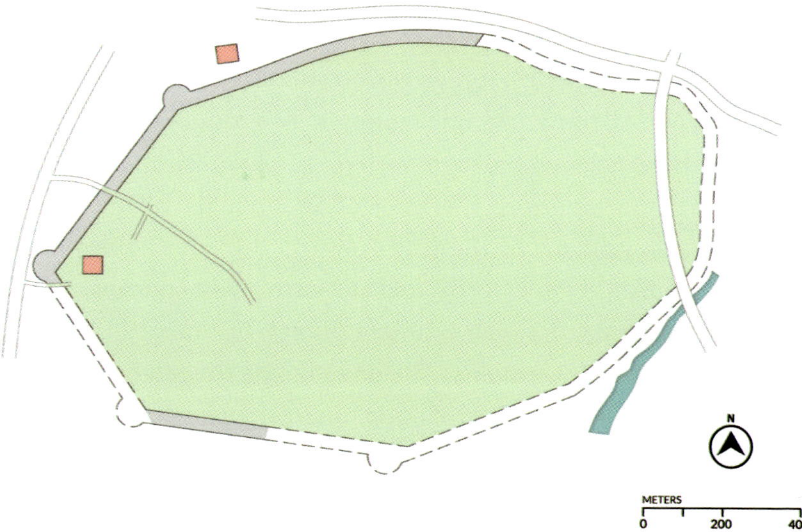

Siri Fort Plan

further taken for Shahjahanabad. There are several mentions, in various records, of buildings like Qasr-e-Hazar-Sutoon (Palace of Thousand Pillars, not to be confused with Bijai Mandal of Muhammad Bin Tughlaq in Malviya Nagar) and Lal Mahal (Red Palace, not to be confused with Lal Mahal of Nizamuddin Basti) situated inside the city. However, the location of these lost buildings is also not known. There is also a possibility that the mentioned Red Palace was inside the walls of Qila-i-Rai Pithora, and not Siri.

Location	Siri Fort area, South Delhi
Period	Khalji
Public Access	Not Applicable (only a tiny portion of wall left, standing along road)
Managing Authority	Archaeological Survey of India
Built by	Ala-ud-Din Khalji
Latitude-Longitude	Not Applicable

NAJAFGARH

LAL DUAR

Some say that Mirza Najaf Khan (1723–82 CE) was the most powerful Mughal General after Aurangzeb. He was a member of the Persian Safvi royalty, which was deposed by the attack of Nadir Shah from Iran. He and many of his relatives were imprisoned by Nadir Shah. The Emperor of Delhi, Muhammad Shah sent an ambassador to Nadir Shah. He was Mirza Muhsin, the elder brother of Nawab Safdarjung of Awadh. Along with other discussions, Mirza Muhsin was also able to negotiate the release of 13-year-old Najaf Khan and his elder sister. The sister was married to Mirza Muhsin and Najaf Khan accompanied the newly-wed couple to Awadh. When Mirza Muhsin died and his son Nawab Muhammad Quli was also murdered by Nawab Shuja-ud-Daula, Najaf Khan came to Delhi to seek service in the court of the Mughal Emperor. Emperor Shah Alam

Previous page: Delhi gate of Najafgarh

appointed him as the Amir-ul-Umra and bestowed the title of Zulfiqaar-ud-Daula upon him. He also took charge to strengthen the Mughal Army and the defence of Delhi. In this process, he built a fort on the outskirts, from where he feared the threat of an attack. This fort was called Najafgarh. The Gazetteer of Rural Delhi published in 1987 mentions Najaf Khan as the Prime Minister of emperor Shah Alam.

Today, Najafgarh is a dense locality in the western end of Delhi, and very few traces of the fort survive. The most prominent surviving structure is the main gate of the fort, opening on the road towards Delhi. It became popular as Delhi Gate. Internally, this gate is a double storeyed structure, with arches opening towards east and west. In between these archways, are the double-storeyed *dalan*s, used for residential purposes. Somewhere in the late 1800s or early 1900s, the lower level *dalan*s were fitted with the gates and rooms were used. When Maulvi Zafar Hasan was preparing his report in the early 1900s, he noted the original Mughal era door panels, fitted with traditional iron nails. Those are nowhere to be seen now. This fort had a gate on each side (North, West, South and East), however, only the western Delhi Gate survives.

In the 1880s, three replacement gates were added on the remaining three sides of the locality. However, post-Independence, during the expansion of the road, those three gates were again demolished. These gates have been built over and over and today very humble modern structures stand there marking the three spots. As of 2020, the eastern gate was being rebuilt.

There used to be a ditch around the Fort wall, which was filled, when the British took over, after the Battle of Najafgarh in 1857. This battle was fought not too far from this fort when the Indian soldiers tried to reach Najafgarh Fort to capture it and attack the British encampment around Delhi from behind. However, to create an illusion, they took a longer route, while the British sensed their intention and reached Najafgarh a few hours before them. In the massive fight on 25 August 1857, around 800 Indian soldiers lost their lives in the battle between Major Nicholson and soldiers from Bareilly, Nimach and Nasirabad. Five citizens of Najafgarh, who tried

Interior of the gateway

to help the Indian soldiers were arrested and hanged in public from a *neem* tree in the middle of the fort. Today, the area where the hanging happened is marked as Jawahar Chowk. A plaque was installed there in 1957 and later a statue of Jawahar Lal Nehru was also installed. The *neem* trees still stand there,

The plaque installed by the British after the World War

and a temple has also come up in the congested chowk. Najafgarh also contributed to the First World War. The plaque installed at the Delhi Gate by the British reads:

> 'From The Zails of Najafgarh, Isapur and Palam 1805 Men Went To the Great War 1914–1919 of These 159 Gave Up Their Lives'

Najaf Khan died on 22 April 1782. He was 49 years old at the time of this death. He was buried near the tomb of Safdarjung and his tomb remains unfinished to date. The tomb's western wall touches Aurobindo

Marg and is next to the Safdarjung Flyover. Its eastern wall contains the entry gate, from the Lodhi Colony side and the North wall is shared by residential quarters in B. K. Dutt colony. The southern wall is next to the railway tracks, connecting several local stations of Delhi.

After the death of Najaf Khan, his property was shared by many. In the British records, we find mention of these buildings. For example, in some records, it is mentioned that the courtroom of Najaf Khan was later converted into a rest house during the British Raj. However, no traces are to be found of that building now. The residence of Najaf Khan was situated along the southern wall of the fort. The British converted this house into a police station. Later the old building was removed, and a new complex came up. Najafgarh's police has been in limelight for its humanitarian work and helping the people, especially during the times of the Covid-19 Pandemic of 2020. Maulvi Zafar Hasan, the British period superintendent of the Archaeological Survey of India for Delhi Circle recorded that the original house was made of *lakhori* bricks (Late Mughal era) and red sandstone. The central courtyard measured 42 x 72 feet, surrounded by arched *dalan*s. There was a 2 feet 4 inches platform on the western side, measuring 72 feet by 13 feet and 10 inches. Further to the west of this platform was a three-arched *dalan* of red sandstone, which was two bays deep and each bay had compartments at either wing. There also used to be a basement under this platform and the *dalan*. The access to the basement was from the northeast side and the southeast corners of the platform. Zafar Hasan also describes a three-chambered *hammam* in the southeast corner of the house and a huge cross-shaped marble tank in the courtyard. The roof of the house had a wall with holes, through which, guns could be fired. In the northeast corner of the house, there were 31 feet wide octagonal towers, which had a well in the centre and a Persian wheel on the top. Through this Persian wheel, the water was fetched into the tank and supplied to the entire house.

When the Marathas occupied Delhi, the Bakshi of Gwalior, Munshi Bhawani Shankar was transferred to Delhi and given a responsible position by the Marathas in the Delhi court. However, he conspired with the British and was removed from his services. The British took care of him and gave him a prime mansion in Shahjahanabad (Old Delhi). His mansion soon became famous as 'Namak Haram ki Haveli' (Mansion of a Traitor). That building in Kuncha Ghisaram is still popular with the same name. Since the people of Old Delhi were not very fond of Bhawani Shankar, he spent some quality time in Najafgarh, where he occupied the residence of Najaf Khan, before it became the police station. He repaired the house and built a row of compartments outside the house, along the northern wall. He also added a few rooms on the roof.

Zafar Hasan also mentions the mosque of Najafgarh, which was situated about 200 yards to the northwest of the Delhi Gate. However, today, there are no traces of the original structure. In the early 1900s, the mosque was the property of one Mir Husain Ali and is marked as an unimportant building from the point of view of archaeological protection/conservation. There was also a small well in the southeast corner of the courtyard. Today, a mosque with the same name, Jami Masjid, exists in Najafgarh, but with a modern structure.

Some 500 yards to the northeast of Delhi Gate (outside the fort), we find the mention of a garden built by Najaf Khan. It was owned by Rati Ram, Bishan Singh and Daud Khan when the British archaeologist prepared his report at the beginning of the 1900s. This garden had a boundary wall, made of bricks, and had octagonal bastions, all in dilapidated condition. It also had the remains of a baradari and some other buildings. By this time, the British had already constructed a Dak Bungalow in the middle of the garden. Tracing the location of this garden, one would reach the area now occupied by the SDM office.

Today, hardly anything of the original times survives. Even the Delhi Gate has been plastered over and layered with modern tiles. This transformation was done in 1999 and the gate was renamed as 'Vad Kishan Lal Duar' [sic]. A plaque on it mentions that Vaid Kishan Lal was a freedom fighter. We have many streets named after him in Najafgarh. However, it was difficult to find more information about him or his work. While strolling through the congested lanes of Najafgarh, one may notice some old buildings, where the plaster is chipped off, and the old Mughal era bricks are exposed. This shows that some walls still survive from the original times. However, there is no documentation of these buildings, and it is difficult to account for them all. One prominent structure is a few metres to the north of the police station (originally Najaf Khan's house). There was an old, locked house, still in its original shape with the old gateway and rooms existing till 2020.

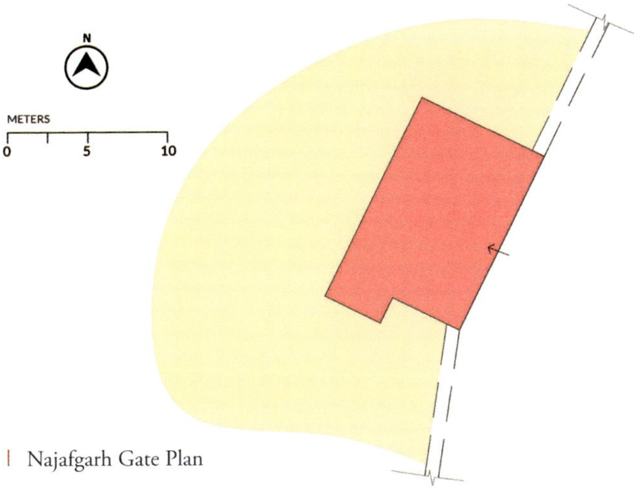

Najafgarh Gate Plan

As this book was being written, workers had started dismantling a portion of the building and a new structure will soon replace it. We do not have information about its origin, or if it was connected to Najaf Khan, Bhawani Shankar, or someone else. No other structure in or around Najafgarh has been marked as protected by State or Centre governments.

Location	Najafgarh locality, West Delhi
Period	Mughal
Public Access	Open (only 1 gate left)
Managing Authority	Local community
Built by	Mirza Najaf Khan
Latitude-Longitude	28.612322733338228, 76.98558794711164

NAI KA KOT

Situated on a small hill, about half a kilometre to the east of the Adilabad Fort, is another fortification, which finds very little mention in the annals of history. Maulvi Zafar Hasan, while preparing his list of Delhi's monuments, mentions it as the 'washerman's, barber's or sweeper's fort'. But Carr Stephen calls it the 'Emperor's Fort' or the 'Right Fort', as it is situated to the right of the fort of emperor Muhammad Bin Tughlaq. Bashir-ud-Din Ahmed in *Waqiaat-i-Dar-ul Huqumat-i-Delhi* does not have a separate head for this Fort. Instead,

Previous page: Northern entry to the Fort

Below: Interior of the Fort

the description of this fort is in continuation to the chapter on Adilabad. Ahmed says that it is the extension of Adilabad and while the latter was the fort of King, this was a garrison for guards. He does not mention the 'Nai ka Kot' name but does say that this fort is called 'Qila Shehenshahi', and 'Dhobi ka Qila' and 'Dahina Qila'. Given the lack of documentation, it remains a mystery, as to how this fort acquired its current name. There is also a possibility that it was called 'Nayak ka Kot', which translates into 'the fort of hero' (read: warrior). The word 'Nayak' could have later corrupted to Nai. But this is only a hypothesis and cannot be proven.

View from the inside of the southeastern entry

The wall of Nai ka Kot is only 200 metres long and the entire structure is in bad shape. Ahmed talks of a market and a small city around this fort. There must have been some settlements between the Nai ka Kot and Adilabad. However, today, this area is clear and at the foothill of the Nai ka Kot, we have a dry dock. The fort has been in ruinous condition for long and this finds mention in the documents of early historians.

Many chroniclers have tried to build fables around this fort. The most common one is that this fort was built by (or for) the barber of Muhammad Bin Tughlaq. R.V. Smith gave a theory that Tughlaq might have used this fort as a retreat when he needed a break from imperial life and only the barber, washerman, and sweeper would have accompanied him; hence the three names. A bridge between Adilabad and Nai Ka Kot also finds a mention in some contemporary blogs, but no such traces were ever found by archaeologists, and even the early historians do not mention any such structure.

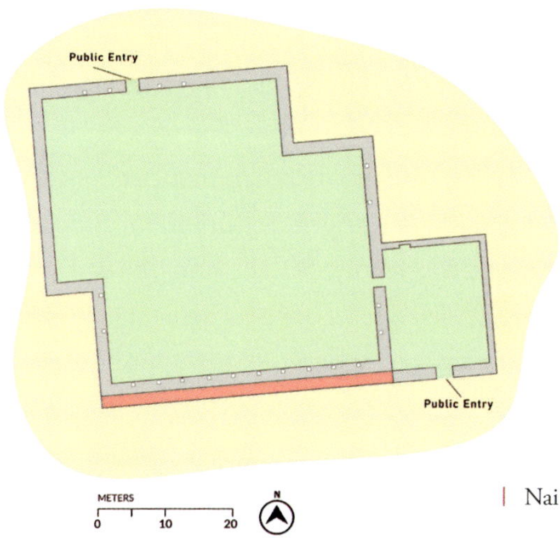

Nai ka Kot Plan

Location	Behind Dry Dock, at Okhla Mod, near Adilabad-Tughlaqabad
Period	Tughlaq
Public Access	Free Entry
Managing Authority	Archaeological Survey of India
Built by	Muhammad Bin Tughlaq
Latitude-Longitude	28.504147285471497, 77.27623592100528

Acknowledgements

When I thought of writing a book, I had initially picked forts as my topic of interest. I soon realised that people usually do not know much about the forts of Delhi beyond Red Fort, Old Fort, and to some extent, Tughlaqabad. The journey for this book has been amazing. The oldest fort I remember enjoying properly is the Fort of Kangra in Himachal Pradesh, where my father, S. Gurdev Singh, had taken me to celebrate my birthday for 3 consecutive years. My love for Delhi's forts started when Sh. K.K. Muhammed, the then Superintending Archaeologist of Delhi Circle, Archaeological Survey of India invited me to his official residence, which was inside the Red Fort. A few days later, I was invited again to see the *baoli* of Red Fort. As I drove through the Delhi Darwaza of the Fort, I noticed those huge, majestic elephants. It struck me that every fort has several hidden secrets that the general public misses. Soon, the work on this book started. But, the process became slow as I moved to write the book on *baoli*s. While I continued to read about forts, I spent more time researching *boalis*. The *baolis* book was released in 2019, and I returned to my original research on forts. Several people helped me in this journey, to whom I would like to extend my gratitude.

As I try to remember the names of all the people who helped me in this journey, my heart sinks, for many of them were taken away by the second wave of COVID-19. One prominent name is Advocate Lakhendra Singh *ji*, who left us in April 2021. He gifted me my first copy of the translation of *Tarikh-i-Firoz Shahi*. The book has immensely helped me understand the Khilji & Tughlaq era. I then approached Rampur Raza Library to pick the facsimile of the old manuscript preserved by them to verify some of the translated elements. Some officers of ASI, who helped me during my study inside the forts also left us in 2020 & '21.

My father, S. Gurdev Singh has always been my strongest support. I would have quit a long ago if it was not for him. Even after taking retirement from his business, he restarted his work, as I wanted to take a long sabbatical to do my research. Every article or book I write, every lecture I give and every site I visit, has been possible because of his blessings. He paints the covers of my books with love. In this world, when a book is judged by its cover, it is his talent that makes my books so special.

One person who cares for me and guides me just like my father is Sh. Sohail Hashmi. I will always remain indebted to him for his selfless guidance. There has not been a time when I turned to him for help and returned empty-handed. He treats my work as his own and takes equal amount of pain in verifying every line I have written. All this, without expecting anything in return, like a true mentor.

Dr Narayani Gupta, Sh. Ratish Nanda, Sh. Janhwij Sharma, Arjun Kumar and Priyank Gupta are a few learned souls, who always help me recharge my thoughts and explore more. They are always an inspiration and just a phone-call away when I need them.

And how can I leave the names of Trisha, Tauseef Ahmed and Gurpreet Virk out of this list? They keep pushing me when I slow down.

My friends through various social media channels have also been a big help. I have posted a lot of queries on Facebook and Twitter and got answers within a matter of hours.

Thank you to everyone, who made this book possible.

References

1. Ahmed, Bashir-ud-din. 1919. *Waqiaat-i-Dar-ul Huqumat-i-Delhi.* Agra: Dar Matba Shamsi.

2. Bernier, Francois. 2010. *Travels in the Mogul Empire*, trans. by Archibald Constable, AES.

3. Cole, Henry Hardy. 1872. *The Architecture of Ancient Delhi: Especially the Buildings Around the Kutb Minar.* London: Arundel Society.

4. Cooper, Frederick. 1865. *The Handbook for Delhi.* Lahore: T.C. McCarthly.

5. Cunningham, Alexander, J.D. Beglar, and A.C.L. Carlleyle. 1874. *Archeological Survey of India: Report for the Year 1871-72: Delhi [and] Agra*. New Delhi: Archaeological Society of India.

6. Harcourt, Alfred Frederick Pollock. 1866. *The New Guide to Delhi*. Allahabad: Pioneer Press.

7. Dutta Sur, Anuradha. 2014. *Lal Kot to Lal Qila: The Architectural Heritage of Delhi*. New Delhi: ABI Prints & Publishing Co.

8. Mani, B.R. 1997. *Delhi - Threshold of the Orient.* New Delhi: Aryan Books International.

9. Khwaja, G.S. 2012. *Islamic Architecture of Delhi.* New Delhi: Bharatiya Kala Prakashan.

10. Hearn, Gordon Risley. 1906. *The Seven Cities of Delhi*. London: 1906

11. Sanderson, Gordon. *Delhi Fort: A Guide to the Buildings and Gardens.* Delhi: Manager of Publications.

12. Fanshaw, H.C. 1902. *Delhi Past and Present.* London: J. Murray.

13. Elliot, H.M. and John Dowson. 2013. *Tarikh-i-Firoz Shahi* of Barani & Afif. First Print 1867. Reprint LPP.

14. Keene, Henry George. 1882. *A Handbook for Visitors to Delhi and its Neighbourhood*. Calcutta: Thacker, Spink & Co.

15. Inventory of Monuments and Sites of National Importance, Delhi Circle. Delhi: Archaeological Society of India.

16. Maulvi Zafar Hasan, *Monuments of Delhi - Lasting Splendour of the Great Mughals and Others*. ASI: 1916

17. Guerrieri, Pilar Maria. 2017. *Maps of Delhi*. New Delhi: Niyogi Books.

18. Nath, R. 2010. *Monuments of Delhi.* Ajmer/Jaipur: The Heritage.

19. Nanda, Ratish and Narayani Gupta. 1999. *Delhi: The Built Heritage: A Listing.* New Delhi: INTACH.

20. Khan, Sir Syed Ahmed. *Asar-us-Sanadid*. Reprint, Urdu Academy: 2014

21. The Delhi Almanac and Souvenir for the Year 1850. Delhi: 1850

22. *The Imperial Gazetteer Atlas of India*. Oxford: 1931

23. Sharma, Y.D. 1964. *Delhi and its Neighbourhood.* New Delhi: Archaeological Society of India.

24. Wheeler, Edmund. 1857. *What shall we do at Delhi?: An Englishman's Letter to the Humanitarians.* London: Daniel F. Oakey.